Halloween:

a GROWN-UP'S GUIDE to

CREATIVE COSTUMES, DEVILISH DECOR & FABULOUS FESTIVITIES

Halloween:

a GROWN-UP'S GUIDE to

CREATIVE COSTUMES, DEVILISH DECOR

& FABULOUS FESTIVITIES

Joanne O'Sullivan

LARK BOOKS

A Division of Sterling Publishing Company, Inc.
NEW YORK

Art Director
SUSAN MCBRIDE

Photography
KEITH WRIGHT
WWW.KEITHWRIGHT.COM

Cover Design
BARBARA ZARETSKY

Photo Illustration
BRIGID BURNS

Assistant Art Directors
HANNES CHAREN
SHANNON YOKELY

Art Intern
LORELEI BUCKLEY

Editorial Assistance
DELORES GOSNELL
ANNE WOLFF HOLLYFIELD
HELENA KNOX
RAIN NEWCOMB

Library of Congress Cataloging-in-Publication Data

O'Sullivan, Joanne.
  Halloween : a grown-up's guide to creative costumes, devilish decor &
fabulous festivities / by Joanne O'Sullivan.— 1st ed.
    p. cm.
Includes index.
  ISBN 1-57990-346-0
  1. Halloween decorations. 2. Halloween costumes. I. Title.
  TT900.H32O84 2003
  745.594'1646—dc21

                                    2002155186

—
10 9 8 7 6 5 4 3 2 1

First Edition

Published by Lark Books, a division of
Sterling Publishing Co., Inc.
387 Park Avenue South, New York, N.Y. 10016

© 2003, Lark Books
Distributed in Canada by Sterling Publishing,
c/o Canadian Manda Group, One Atlantic Ave., Suite 105
Toronto, Ontario, Canada M6K 3E7

Distributed in the U.K. by:
Guild of Master Craftsman Publications Ltd.
Castle Place
166 High Street
Lewes
East Sussex
England
BN7 1XU
Tel: (+ 44) 1273 477374
Fax: (+ 44) 1273 478606
Email: pubs@thegmcgroup.com
Web: www.gmcpublications.com

Distributed in Australia by Capricorn Link (Australia) Pty Ltd., P.O. Box 704,
Windsor, NSW 2756 Australia

If you have questions or comments about this book, please contact:
Lark Books
67 Broadway
Asheville, NC 28801
(828) 236-9730

Manufactured in Hong Kong

ISBN 1-57990-346-0

Contents

Introduction

When you were a kid, it was all about the candy. Years later, you can still remember the excitement of getting your favorite chocolate bar in spades, and the bitter disappointment of discovering that once again, your neighbors were giving out nothing but those inferior-quality taffy things. You may have created elaborate cataloguing systems for your candy—chocolates under the bed, lollipops in your sock drawer—or a byzantine barter system with your siblings—four dark chocolate miniatures in exchange for amnesty from a day's chores.

Now that you're a grown-up, you can buy your own candy—as much as you want, whenever you want. So why is Halloween still your favorite holiday? Maybe it's because Halloween puts us in touch with the magical—

something that's notably absent in our sensible grown-up lives. As the sun goes down and the chilly fall wind whips leaves around in an eerie dance, even the most level-headed adults must admit that there's something in the air on Halloween night, a ghost of a chance that there may be, well, a ghost or two hovering about. Perhaps it's because on this night, even a grown-up can break free from a polished appearance and a poised demeanor to become, for just one night, an enchanted being, a terrifying beast, or a sultry sorceress. Or maybe it's because Halloween is the one holiday that's all about fun, pure and simple. There are no presents to buy, no stressful family dynamics to deal with, no giant dinner to cook—just playing dress-up, and enjoying time with friends.

Since kids and grown-ups love Halloween for different reasons, we thought it was about time there

was a Halloween guide with a decidedly adult approach to the holiday. Let the kids run door-to-door for candy. You can celebrate in your own uniquely grown-up way. Dress up or deck the halls in orange and black. Hold a fabulous fête that will keep your friends talking until New Year's Eve. We've got all the ideas you need right here.

If you're looking for costume inspiration, we offer new designs and some fresh interpretations of old standbys. These costumes were designed just for adults, so when you wear them you'll look original and creative, not like an overgrown trick-or-treater. If sewing isn't part of your skills set, don't despair. You can put together a sensational costume without so much as looking at a sewing machine. Basic black clothes or linens that you already have in your closet serve as a foundation. We'll show you how to transform them into inventive costumes that

will make an instant impression.
Your office or garage may hold a
treasure trove of unconventional
materials, too, and we'll explain how
you can use them for great results.
If you're spending Halloween night
as part of a couple, you'll find ideas
for couples costumes and clever
theme costume ideas for parties.

If you're too timid to make a whole
costume, don a mask, paint your face,
or put on a hat. We offer clever ideas
that can enhance your costume or
serve as costumes all by themselves.

Decorating your home or yard for
Halloween can help get you in the
holiday spirit, so we've come up with
unique ideas to inspire you.
Pumpkins are a must for Halloween,
but they don't always need to sport
smiling faces. The pumpkin projects
we suggest will help you take a
fresh look at the familiar
orange globe, and breathe

new life into an old tradition.
Beyond pumpkins, you'll find suggestions for creating yard figures,
window and mantle treatments, and
seasonal tableaus. With looks ranging
from eek to chic, you'll find something to suit your style.
And finally, there are parties, the

area in which grown-ups arguably
excel over kids. You've done the
apple bobbing and the caramel
popcorn balls. Why not try something more sophisticated this
Halloween? We suggest three themes
with full party plans, from the invitations to the ambience and activities. You can follow the plan entirely or use the ideas as a springboard
for your own enchanted evening of
entertainment.

Halloween is almost here.
Tap into the magic that's in the air
and celebrate this bewitching holiday with a kid's enthusiasm and a
grown up's sense of style.

The History of Halloween

Halloween is a hodge-podge of holidays and autumnal traditions with roots dating back thousands of years. Through each new era in time, and with each culture that has observed it, this holiday has been re-interpreted and re-emerged with a new meaning.

Most historians trace the source of the modern-day Halloween to the ancient Celts of the British Isles, an agrarian people who divided the year into only two seasons: summer and winter. At summer's end, they held a festival called Samhain (pronounced sow-in), essentially a Celtic New Year's celebration. Samhain was a time to celebrate the harvest, acknowledge the past, and look toward the future. Those who had died in the past year were remembered, and food was left for their spirits, which were said to be present as the year changed. Since looking into the future was important, priests practiced divination rituals. On Samhain night, all home fires were extinguished to represent the end of the year. A huge new fire was built by Celtic priests (known as Druids) and everyone re-lit their hearth fires with embers from the sacred fire. It is said that Celts carried the embers from the sacred fire back to their home in hollowed out turnips, a precursor to the jack-o'lantern lighting tradition.

The Celts believed that the transition from the old year to the new created a sort of wrinkle in time; events that took place on this night existed outside of real time. At this crucial crossroads between past and present, magical creatures such as fairies were especially active. The fairy mounds (underground fairy colonies) were open on Samhain, and fairies were free to come out and create all manner of mischief. Humans needed to protect themselves from tricky fairies, so some believe that wearing disguises to confuse the fairies may have been

part of the Samhain rituals, and this may be how costumes became part of Halloween traditions.

As time went on, invaders brought other cultures to the British Isles. In 43 A.D, the Romans came along and stayed for almost 400 years. They brought their own autumn festivals with them, and eventually Celtic and Roman traditions started to overlap. The Romans celebrated Paternalia, a festival honoring the dead, in October, and on November 1, they honored Pomona, the goddess of fruit and trees. Pomona was represented holding an apple, and the festival involved playing games involving fruits and nuts. Halloween traditions such as bobbing for apples have their roots in this Roman custom.

As Christianity took hold in Britain and Ireland around the seventh century, the Church sought to separate their converts from their pre-Christian beliefs. The Church developed a new spin on the nature spirits and gods that the Celts and Romans had believed in. They were recast as demons, devils, and witches. Since new Christians wanted to distance themselves from such negative images, they abandoned the old festivals and began to celebrate the new holy days that the church created, Hallowmas or Allhallows, now known as All Saints' Day on November 1

and All Souls' Day on November 2. The Church preserved the Roman practice of honoring the dead, but added the saints as well as the ancestors. The night before these holy days became known as All Hallows' Eve, All Hallow e'en, and eventually Halloween.

For centuries, people in the British Isles developed their own regional interpretations of these holidays. To replace the ancient practice of leaving food and wine for spirits on Samhain, the church encouraged the distribution of "soul cakes" on All Soul's Day. Working-class children went from door to door "souling" on November 1, begging for soul cakes in exchange for promises to pray for the dead. Divination still remained a part of the holiday, too. In some parts of Britain and Ireland, Halloween was called Nutcrack Night or Snap Apple Night because of the divination games people played. Young girls labeled nuts, one for each potential suitor, then threw them into the fire. The nut that cracked represented her future husband. Snap Apple was a game in which apples were suspended

from the ceiling by strings. The first person to grasp an apple with her teeth would be the first to marry. The holiday was primarily a quaint family celebration with none of the ghoulish associations it holds today.

In the nineteenth century, immigration brought people from the British Isles to the United States in great numbers, and with them they brought their traditions, including Halloween. By this time, Halloween had lost its religious significance and had once again become a folk holiday. Each new generation created a Halloween that reflected the popular culture of the time. A Victorian Halloween reflected the preoccupation with romance so common in that era, and divination games were the primary activities of the evening. Halloween was more like Valentine's Day, so it was seen as the province of singles, especially young women. Since no one believed in fairies anymore, it was up to young boys to make mischief. They overturned outhouses, broke windows, and sometimes got into serious trouble.

Sometime around the turn of the twentieth century, the tide began to turn, and Halloween became a holiday for children.

The practice of souling had been reinterpreted as trick-or-treating door to door for candy. To appeal to children rather than scare them, ghosts were depicted as friendly, and jack-o'lanterns had smiling faces. When the cultural tide turned again in the 1970s, children were warned of the possible dangers in their candy bags. Rumors of contaminated candy circulated, and although they were later proven false, parents no longer felt safe sending their children to their neighbors' doors. Fundamentalist Christian groups decried Halloween as a devil-worshiping holiday and started a campaign to outlaw it. At the same time, Hollywood started churning out "slashers" which promoted the idea of Halloween as a dangerous time when deranged humans, not spirits, roam the streets with murderous intent.

As the cultural pendulum slowly swings back again, Halloween has once again become a holiday celebrated by both children and adults. It has begun to move back across the Atlantic to the countries of its origin in a new form and has crossed the US borders into Mexico and Canada. It's anybody's guess how this holiday will be reinvented as it spreads to other cultures and is discovered by new generations.

Costumes

Our busy grown-up lives offer very few opportunities to act against type. And then, once a year, Halloween night comes along, and all bets are off. You've got carte blanche to be anyone or anything. You want to look creative. You want to look great. And you've only got one night, so you'd better make it good.

If you're usually serious, be outrageous. If you're usually cheerful, be scary. Be what no one would ever expect. We offer ideas beyond the plastic, packaged costumes you find in stores. After all, your costume reflects who you are. Do you really want to be something that came out of the bargain bin?

Peruse the ideas in the following section.

Be inspired.

Contest-Winning Costumes

If you are going to make a costume for Halloween, why not go all out? The costumes in this section are sure to win admiring comments whether or not you enter a contest. You won't need weeks to make them—just the right materials and a whole lot of attitude.

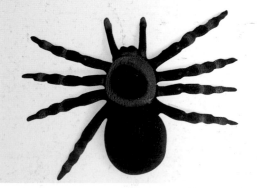

BLACK WIDOW SPIDER

For a really scary Halloween evening, be an eight-legged enchantress in this black widow spider costume. When your date picks you up, recite interesting facts about the black widow. Note that black widows are the most venomous spiders in North America and that females are usually shy, nocturnal creatures that don't like to leave their webs. Mention that it is true that females do eat their mates after mating, but that if they are well fed, they will allow their mate to live for another day. This should score you dinner at a nice restaurant. Along with your four-legged "spiderpack" wear a black leotard, tights, hat, and gloves.

YOU WILL NEED

FOAM PIPE INSULATION TUBES*
SCISSORS
BLACK FAUX FUR
MEDIUM-WEIGHT CARDBOARD
BLACK VELVETEEN
HOT GLUE GUN AND GLUE STICKS
HEAVY-GAUGE WIRE
WIRE CUTTER
WORK GLOVES
COTTON OR POLYESTER FIBERFILL
BLACK ELASTIC BANDING
PLASTIC ORNAMENT BALLS**
STRONG, SOFT BLACK YARN
RED CRAFT FELT

*Available at hardware stores
**Available at craft stores

Costume by Trulee Grace Hall

FOR THE SPIDER LEGS

1. The legs on your "spiderpack" are made from foam insulation tubing. It's lightweight so it won't hurt your back to wear them, and it's usually sold in several lengths. We used two 6-foot (1.8 m) lengths and cut them in half to make four 3-foot-long (91.4 cm) legs.

2. Cut black faux fur covers for the foam legs. Hold a piece of the fur around one leg to determine how much you'll need to cover it. Hot glue the fabric to the tube, stuffing any extra fur into the hollow tube. Cut a small round cover for one end of the tube and leave the other end open. Repeat for the other tube legs.

3. Cut an oblong piece of cardboard to fit on the center of your back (this is the frame for your spiderpack). Cut a piece of faux fur to the same size, adding a 1-inch (2.5 cm) border all around and set this piece aside.

11. Attach the furry legs to the pack by sliding a leg down each wire. You can bend the wire for better spider leg positions. Attach the legs to the pack with hot glue so that they are securely in place and don't slide off.

12. Cut two elastic straps to reach from the top of your spiderpack, around your shoulder, and down to the bottom of pack. Attach these straps as though you were preparing a backpack. The top of the straps will be positioned on the spider back so that the straps sit between your shoulder blades. They will reach around your shoulders and attach to the bottom of back close together, near the bottom of your spine. Hot glue the straps to the pack and sew over them for extra strength if you can.

13. The spider eyes are made from plastic ornament balls, made for sewing craft projects. The mesh pattern on the surface of the balls is wide enough so that you can see through it. Pull the balls apart and spray paint each side whatever color you imagine the eyes to be (red is very striking). Tie a piece of yarn through one of the mesh holes on each side of the ball. Position each side over one of your eyes to find out how long the center piece of yarn (that will go over your nose) should be. Once you've determined a length, thread the yarn through the half-sphere, making little knots inside. Add two long pieces of yarn on the sides to pull back and tie at the back of your head.

14. Cut a red hourglass shape from felt and attach it to your leotard with masking tape.

4. Cut a piece of velveteen material about the same shape as the cardboard piece, but with a 6-inch (15.2 cm) border all around. This piece will be the hump of your spiderpack.

5. Cut two long pieces of the heavy-gauge wire, each just under the length of your arm's span. The wire will serve as the structural support for your furry legs and will be attached to the cardboard shape. Decide where you'd like the legs to be positioned on your back.

6. Wearing work gloves to protect your hands, poke the wire through the cardboard near the edge, then pull it across back of the shape and out through the other side.

7. Make four holes in the large velveteen fabric hump piece, near the edges. Pull the wire through these holes, so that four pieces of wire stick out, positioned to hold the weight of the legs.

8. Hot glue the velveteen hump piece to the back side of the cardboard, leaving an opening so you can insert the stuffing.

9. Stuff the hump with fiberfill, pushing it in until you have a plump pillow shape. Add extra stuffing around the wires so that they don't cut into your back.

10. Hot glue the round furry piece that you cut in step 3 to the exposed back piece of cardboard.

DANCING QUEEN

You can dance, you can jive. Have the time of your life. You are the dancing queen. Even if you're no longer young, sweet, or 17, on Halloween night, the ABBA fairy waves her magic wand and gives everyone a chance to be the dancing queen.

This dazzling disco fantasy costume is a piece of cake to make. Gather a pile of free software CDs, starting with the ones you're constantly getting in the mail, then begging for more from your office IT person, who will probably be more than willing to part with them.

Drill a hole in each side of each CD (the holes should be roughly at 12 o'clock, 3 o'clock, 6 o'clock, and 9 o'clock). String the CDs together with thin, clear, plastic cord (obviously you will have made sure that it fits through the holes). For our costume, we used three rows of seven CDs each for the front and two rows of five CDs each for the back (even the dancing queen has to sit down sometimes, so we left off the back middle panel). Tie your two back panels together with a piece of cord running across your back.

Wear all white under your CD dress. Spray paint a pair of boots silver for footwear. Wear disco ball earrings and carry a tambourine. If you've got a date for Halloween night, suggest a Fernando costume so you can be the all-ABBA twosome.

SAMURAI WARRIOR

If you're really a fraidy cat in your day-to-day life, Halloween is your chance to be a fearless warrior, like a samurai. This costume is made mostly of joss paper, a specialty Asian paper used to roll incense. You can find heaps of it in any Asian grocery store, and it's quite inexpensive. In the center of each piece of joss paper is a shiny square of metallic leaf, either silver or gold. Pieced together, it looks like panels of samurai armor. If you don't have access to joss paper, try spray painting cardboard silver to achieve the same look.

YOU WILL NEED

JOSS PAPER*
SCISSORS
STAPLER AND STAPLES
RIBBON OR ½-INCH (1.3 CM) WIDE BIAS TAPE
POSTER BOARD
SPRAY ADHESIVE
ALUMINUM FLASHING
BALLPOINT PEN
BLACK BASEBALL CAP
HOT GLUE GUN AND GLUE STICKS

*Sold in large, inexpensive packets at Asian grocery stores

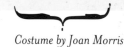

Costume by Joan Morris

FOR THE SKIRT

1. Start with the long panel that hangs down the center front of the costume. You'll need to trim the plain borders of the joss paper to about ½ inch (1.3 cm) from the metallic square in the center. This panel uses seven pieces of paper, but you may use more or less depending on your height.

2. Start stapling together the pieces on the long center panel. You'll be stapling all the pieces together vertically, like in figure 1. You'll need to start with the bottom square and staple along the top of the squares so that you can hide the staples under the next layer you add.

3. When you've got the center panel done, you can start on the rest of the panels for the skirt. The number of panels you need and their length is dependent on your width and height. For this skirt, we used six panels of five squares each. Each vertical panel is stapled together with the same process used in step 2.

4. Lay all the panels on a flat surface with the long center panel in the middle. Start stapling the panels together by overlapping them. The top square of each panel should be stapled to the adjacent square in the center so that the staples are hidden by the overlap. The rest of the squares can hang loose.

5. Once all the top squares are stapled together, staple a black ribbon horizontally across the top squares to serve as a belt. Make sure it's long enough to fit around your waist and tie.

6. Staple a series of squares over the black ribbon to hide it.

FOR THE CHEST PIECE

1. Lay out the pieces of paper in the shape shown in figure 3. Starting at the bottom, staple them together so that the staples stay hidden.

2. To add strength at the shoulder area, attach the squares to the poster board with spray adhesive before you staple them to the top of the chest piece.

3. Cut two pieces of ribbon and staple one piece to each shoulder. Make it long enough to tie in back or loop under your arms and tie in front.

4. Cover the ribbon on the shoulder area by adding two additional squares of joss paper.

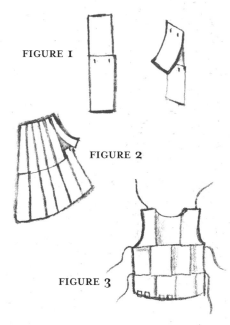

FIGURE 1

FIGURE 2

FIGURE 3

FOR THE HAT

Draw the samurai emblem on a piece of aluminum flashing and cut it out carefully with scissors. Cut out additional aluminum circles and hot glue them to the bill of the cap. Glue the emblem to the bill of a black baseball with the hot glue gun. Accordion pleat six pieces of joss paper and staple four of the pieces to the side edge of the cap and the two remaining pieces above them on the cap.

See page 73 for instructions on making the machete.

Faux Fur Fifi,
THE FRENCH POODLE

Ooo-la-la! **If you wear this costume to a contest, you're bound to get "Best in Show." Fifi has come straight from the doggie beauty parlor with a fresh haircut and she's ready to show it off. Along with a dog collar, you'll need to accessorize this costume with a lot of attitude. Paint a snout and whiskers on your face, and get ready to be the center of attention.**

YOU WILL NEED

WHITE BODY SUIT

UPHOLSTERY FOAM*

SCISSORS

FAUX FUR

MEDIUM-GAUGE WIRE

WIRE CUTTERS OR PLIERS

COTTON OR POLYESTER FIBERFILL

NEEDLE AND STRONG INVISIBLE
THREAD OR FISHING LINE

HOT GLUE GUN AND GLUE STICKS
(OPTIONAL)

KNIT CAP

GLOVES OR MITTENS

SLIPPERS

DOG COLLAR

*Available at fabric stores

Costume by Trulee Grace Hall

1. Start with the tail, which is the only piece that needs to be attached to the bodysuit. Cut a cylindrical shape from the foam. It should be about 2 to 3 inches (5.1 to 7.6 cm) long and about 1¹/₂-inches (3.2 cm) wide.

2. Cut a piece of wire about 6 inches (15.2 cm) longer than the foam cylinder. Poke the wire through the middle of the foam, allowing it to extend out on both ends. On one end, bend the wire into a spiral, and hot glue it to the bodysuit in the appropriate position (you may need to try the bodysuit on and mark the spot). Roll a small tuft of faux fur into a ball (tucking it under and gluing it in place if necessary), and hot glue it to the other end of the wire.

3. To make the poodle "vest," measure from your shoulders to just below your rib cage, then double that measurement, and cut a piece of faux fur to that size (use one of your everyday shirts as a guide for determining the width). Fold the piece in half and cut an opening for your head in the center of the fold line. Pull the piece over your head and figure out where you need to bind up the sides for a tight, but comfortable fit. Mark where the bottom of your arm openings should be and any places where you need to cut off excess fabric for a smooth fit.

4. Hand stitch the sides of the vest closed with strong thread or fishing line. You could also hot glue the sides closed if you're not comfortable with sewing.

5. Wrap a piece of fur around your wrist to get the approximate length and width measurement. The fur should fit snugly, but you've got to be able to get the tuft over your hand. Follow the same process to decide on the measurements for the ankle tufts. When you're satisfied with the measurements, cut the tufts. They should resemble oversized, puffy arm tufts and leg warmers.

6. Sew or hot glue the long edges of the tufts together. Stuff a little fiberfill into the tube you created, then stitch or glue the two short sides together to form a ring.

7. The thigh tufts are constructed like the wrist and ankle tufts. Fit them to your thighs, making sure they're tight enough to stay in place.

Sew or glue the long edges together. When stuffing the tufts, however, don't overstuff. Otherwise your thigh tufts will rub together, making it difficult to walk. When you're finished stuffing, sew or hot glue the short ends closed to form a ring. If you find it easier, and less restrictive, you can glue all the tufts into place on the bodysuit, although the vest will certainly have to come over your head as a separate piece.

8. The cap serves as a base for the head and ears. For the ears, simply cut an ear shape from fur that will be draped over the top of your head. They should be long enough to hang past your jaw line and can be lined with pink faux fur if you wish (cut the pink fur to the same size as the ears and glue the two pieces wrong sides together). Hot glue or sew the top of the ears to the top of the cap.

9. Ball up a bunch of fur (similar to the tail ball, only larger) to serve as a head tuft. Glue or sew the tuft to the front of the cap.

10. When you put on your tufts, be sure that the seams fall on the inside of your arms and legs where you will not see them. As a finishing touch, add a dog collar and slippers in a color to match the rest of your ensemble. You can paint paws onto them with fabric paint if you like.

Finis!

GLADIATOR

If you've got a nice pair of legs, show them off with this gladiator costume. If you're more skilled with a sword than a sewing machine, not to worry. This is a no-sew costume, held together mostly with hot glue. Make sure you wear something underneath, as the "skirt" on the bottom is too revealing even for the most ardent exhibitionist.

YOU WILL NEED

Measuring tape

Brown vinyl, about 2 yards (1.8 m)

Marker

Scissors

Brown spray paint (optional)

Aluminum flashing

Hot glue gun and glue sticks

Awl or ice pick

Leather cord

Costume by Joan Morris

FOR THE SKIRT

1. Measure, mark, and cut a piece of brown vinyl for the skirt. You'll want the piece to fit around your waist and to right about your knees. If the underside of the vinyl is white, then spray paint it brown so that it blends.

2. Measure and mark in two spots: about 4 inches (10.2 cm) in and 2 inches (5.1 cm) down from one long edge of the vinyl. Starting at the opposite long edge, cut up to the mark to create a loose strip. Continue cutting strips vertically up the fabric this way to create the skirt's fringe. When you get to the center of the fabric, make a few of the strips a bit thinner.

3. Cut 2 inches (5.1 cm) off the bottom of all of the strips except thinner strips in the front middle. Trim the rest of the strips into a point at the bottom.

4. Cut small squares from the aluminum flashing (make sure they're not too big to fit on the strips of the skirt. Hot glue them to the strips (except for the long thin ones in the front).

5. Cut aluminum flashing circles to fit on the thin front strips, then glue them to the strips.

6. Poke holes with an awl or ice pick at the top back of the skirt and thread leather cord through the holes to lace the skirt closed.

FOR THE SHIRT

1. Start the shirt by cutting four pieces of vinyl, each long enough to fit comfortably around your mid-section and about 5 inches (12.7 cm) wide. Hot glue the strips together on the long edges to form a tiered, layered piece.

2. Fold a piece of vinyl in half and figure out how big a piece you'll need to create a neck piece that reaches from just over your ribs, over your shoulders, then down to the end of your shoulder blades. Cut a piece to this width, then shape the sides of the fabric as you see in the picture above. Hot glue the four-layered piece to the bottom of this neckpiece.

3. Cut four pieces of vinyl to attach to the edge of the neckpiece as sleeves. The pieces should just cover your shoulders and flare out a bit. Hot glue two pieces to each other as a cap sleeve, then hot glue the sleeve to the edge of the neckpiece. Repeat for the other side.

4. Cut an opening through the front center of the top so that you can get into it. Cut narrow strips of vinyl and hot glue one end of each strip to one side of the opening you cut.

5. Use an awl or ice pick to poke a hole in the unattached end of each strip you cut. Poke a corresponding hole in the shirt, right under the hole you poked in the narrow strip. Cut a piece of leather cord for each strip and lace it through the holes to hold the shirt closed.

6. Decorate the edges of the neckpiece with little cut squares of aluminum flashing attached with hot glue.

ACCESSORIES

Sandals
Wear regular sandals and wrap long strips of vinyl up your calves to imitate Roman sandals. Tape the ends of the vinyl together to keep the straps in place.

Sword
See page 73 for instructions.

Shield
The shield is made from a silver party platter. The ornament in the middle is a curtain tieback hot glued to the platter. The gold nail design is made from flat-backed marbles spray painted gold and hot glued to the platter. Create a strap on the back with a piece of duct tape. Lay two pieces of duct tape (one longer than the other) together, centering the shorter one on top of the larger one, sticky sides together. Attach the sticky part that didn't get covered to the back of the platter.

WINGED THINGS

For filmy wings fit for a fairy or any other magical winged creature, try this technique. The diaphanous look is achieved with iridescent wrapping paper that's laminated in a pouch laminator. These wings are as light as air and catch the light as you flit through the room.

YOU WILL NEED

LARGE PIECE OF POSTER BOARD
MARKER
1 YARD (91.4 CM) OF IRIDESCENT CELLOPHANE WRAPPING PAPER
SCISSORS
11 x 17-INCH (27.9 x 43.2 CM) POUCH LAMINATOR*
26-GAUGE SILVER FLORAL WIRE
STRAIGHT PINS
SEWING MACHINE WITH HEAVY-WEIGHT NEEDLE
NEEDLE AND INVISIBLE THREAD (OPTIONAL)

*Available at copy service centers

Wings by Diana Light

1. Refer to pictures of dragonflies or fairies to decide on the shape for your wings. Remember that each wing will need to fit inside the 11 x 17-inch (27.9 x 43.2 cm) laminator, so be sure to make each smaller than that. Draw each wing separately on a piece of poster board to make templates.

2. Crinkle the iridescent wrapping paper into a ball and then flatten it back out.

3. Use the template as a guide to cut each wing shape separately from the wrapping paper. Cut them slightly smaller than the template size so you'll have a 1/4-inch (6 mm) laminate border after you run the wings through the laminator.

4. Take the wings to the nearest pouch laminator (if you have one at work, all the better) and carefully lay one of the wings inside it.

5. Use floral wire to make the veins in the wings. Just cut it into pieces to fit on top of the wing and position them in a vein pattern.

6. Send the wing through the laminator. Repeat the process for the other wing.

7. Trim the excess lamination from around the wing, leaving just a small border around the cellophane wing.

8. Put on your costume and have a friend pin the wings to the back of it with the straight pins. Stitch the wings onto the costume using a basting stitch on the sewing machine or hand sew them in position.

VARIATION

If you'd prefer to be a bee, or a ladybug, or a fly on the wall, use black plastic mesh screening (used for screen doors and windows) over an iridescent cellophane wing to imitate the texture of insect wings.

After you cut your wing template, use it to create one set of wings from cellophane and two sets from plastic mesh screen. Sandwich the iridescent wing piece between the two layers of the mesh wings. Create a wing shape from 20-gauge floral wire, attached end-to-end and reinforced with floral tape. Bind the layers (mesh, wire, wrapping paper, mesh) of each wing together with electrical tape, or hot glue and bias tape. Use a strong wire to connect the wings, making sure that they're at least a finger's breadth apart.

Attach a ribbon to the strong wire in the center of the wings to act as a harness that you'll run over your shoulders and under your arms. Adjust the wings on your back so that they sit where you want them to, and safety pin the ribbon to the rest of your costume so that they don't move. If you choose not to use a harness for the wings, you can simply stitch or safety pin them directly onto your costume.

FLYING UNDER RADAR

FAIRY FOLK & OTHER MAGICAL PEOPLE

Not all creatures of legend were meant to inspire fear. On the lighter side of the otherworldly spectrum are the goodly mystical creatures. They could be a little mischievous, and sometimes downright mean, but generally they were there to enchant humans, not to eat them.

FAIRIES

There are many different kinds of fairies in different cultural traditions. Generally, they are tiny, ethereal, winged creatures that are only visible in the blink of an eye. In Ireland, fairies are called the Gentry; the Scots call them the Good People, the Good Neighbors, or the Wee Folk; and in Wales, they're called the Tylwyth Teg. There are subterranean fairies and woodland fairies, solitary fairies like the Irish gean-canach (love talker), or "trooping" fairies that wear green jackets and love hunting and riding. Fairies travel on leys or fairy routes which humans should avoid lest they be kidnapped. At night they dance around fairy rings marked by red and white mushrooms growing in a circle in the woods. Fairy behavior ranges from benevolent to treacherous. They are generally kind unless provoked and can help humans if they're so inclined or if bribed with sweetened milk.

SPRITES

Sprites are similar to fairies but live in water. They are said to change the colors of the trees with the change of seasons, and Jack Frost is also said to be a sprite.

GNOMES

Gnomes were known as the Earth elementals, responsible for protecting the treasures of the earth. Found in Scandinavian myth, gnomes are depicted as ugly little people wearing tight-fitting brown clothes and hoods that lived underground. Gnomes are wonderful metal workers, especially of swords and armor. Despite their off-putting physically appearance, gnomes are usually seen as good-natured, hard working, and reliable. In the world of mythical creatures, they are distinguished by their adherence to vegetarianism, although there is no evidence that they were completely vegan.

PIXIES

Pixies are tricky creatures that live in England and look like humans except for their bright red hair and green eyes. They have upturned noses and mischievous smiles and wear tight-fitting green clothes. They can change their size but are usually quite tiny. Pixies like to lead humans astray but can be fooled when people wear their coats inside out. They like to dance on fireplaces.

NYMPHS

In Greek and Roman mythology, nymphs were beautiful women who were minor deities. They inhabited and personified features of nature such as trees, waters, and mountains.

ALSEIDS
Nymphs of the glens and groves

AULONIADS
Nymphs of the pastures

DRYADS
Dryads were responsible for looking out for the well-being of oak trees. If a tree was destroyed, the dryad would die. Dryads punished mortals for damaging trees, so it's a great costume for tree-huggers.

LEIMONIADS
Nymphs of flowers and meadows

MAENADS
Not really nymphs, maenads were the followers of Dionysus. They were spirits of the vineyard and were said to be able to create a stream of wine by tapping the ground with a stick.

NEREID
Nereids were responsible for the well-being of the sea. The nereids could help those lost at sea or cause storms to thwart evildoers or enemies of the Greeks.

FROTHY FAIRY FROCK & HEADPIECE

Since few people have ever actually seen a fairy, you have creative license to wear whatever you want when impersonating one for Halloween. In Emma Pearson's imagination, they look something like this. The lovely layered effect you see in this dress is achieved by spray painting through a piece of lace, then adding layers of tulle on top. Sprinkle everything with a heaping helping of fairy dust (also known as glitter) so that you'll sparkle when you catch the light. Top your frock with a sparkly crown-like headpiece, and don't forget the wings on page 23.

YOU WILL NEED

SLIP OR NIGHTGOWN
DOILY
PIECE OF SCRAP LACE OR CURTAIN
SILVER SPRAY PAINT
STAPLER AND STAPLES
WHITE TULLE
SAFETY PINS
RIBBON OR COLORED TULLE
SEQUINS OR RHINESTONES
HOT GLUE GUN AND GLUE STICKS
GLITTER
PIECE OF PLIABLE WOODY VINE,
SUCH AS GRAPEVINE
FLORIST WIRE OR THIN GAUGE CRAFT
WIRE
WIRE SNIPS
BEADS OR BUTTONS
SCISSORS
SILVER RIBBON

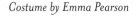

Costume by Emma Pearson

1. Place the slip on a flat surface. Lay a piece of lace or a doily on top of it and spray paint through the lace to create a lace stencil. Let dry.

2. Staple a strip of lace (that you haven't painted through) around the bottom of the slip to make it ankle length.

3. Pin the tulle around the bottom edge of the bra area, including the back, to form a layer over the skirt of the slip.

4. Hot glue ribbon or colored tulle over the safety pins to hide them.

5. Hot glue sequins or rhinestones in a pattern of your choice in the bra area of the slip and on the tulle overlayer. Sprinkle glitter over the entire costume.

FOR THE HEADPIECE

1. Hold a piece of grapevine to your head and cut it to fit your head. Twist the vine into a circle.

2. Using the wire snips, cut a piece of the floral wire about the same length as the vine. Wrap the wire around the vine several times to make sure it doesn't unwind.

3. Cut several 1-yard (91.4 cm) pieces of floral wire. Wrap one wire a few times around the headpiece and then leave about 1 inch (2.5 cm) of wire sticking up. Thread beads or buttons onto the wire, then make a knot in the wire to secure the embellishment, and loop it back down onto the headpiece, wrapping it around several times to secure it. Continue adding embellishments in this manner. For variety, stagger the height of the embellished loops or bend them in opposing directions.

4. Wrap silver ribbon around the headpiece and tie it at the back. Add a few more pieces of silver ribbon to flow down from the headpiece to the back of the neck.

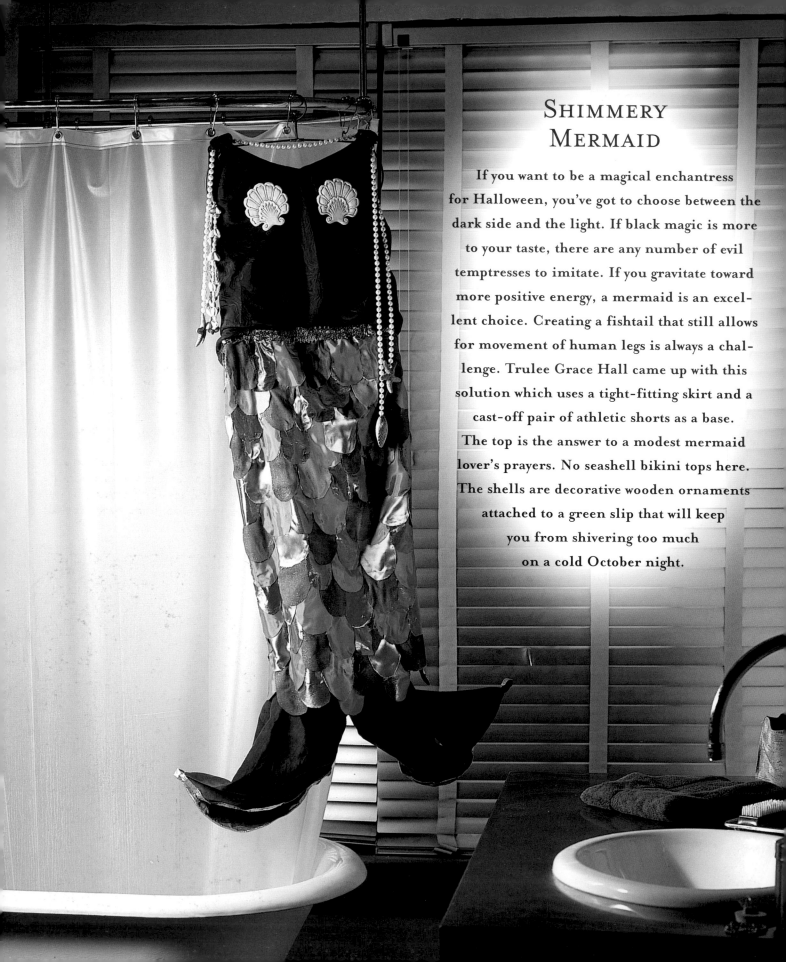

SHIMMERY MERMAID

If you want to be a magical enchantress for Halloween, you've got to choose between the dark side and the light. If black magic is more to your taste, there are any number of evil temptresses to imitate. If you gravitate toward more positive energy, a mermaid is an excellent choice. Creating a fishtail that still allows for movement of human legs is always a challenge. Trulee Grace Hall came up with this solution which uses a tight-fitting skirt and a cast-off pair of athletic shorts as a base. The top is the answer to a modest mermaid lover's prayers. No seashell bikini tops here. The shells are decorative wooden ornaments attached to a green slip that will keep you from shivering too much on a cold October night.

YOU WILL NEED

SEVERAL GREEN FABRIC REMNANTS
IN DIFFERENT TEXTURES,
PREFERABLY SHIMMERY

SCISSORS

TIGHT-FITTING SKIRT

BAGGY, ELASTIC-WAIST ATHLETIC
SHORTS

HOT GLUE GUN AND GLUE STICKS

GOLD ELASTIC SEQUIN TRIM

DECORATIVE WOODEN SHELL SHAPES
OR CRAFT FOAM SHELLS*

SHELL JEWELRY OR FAUX PEARLS

*Used for embellishing mantelpieces or
wooden borders in homes, these can be
found in home improvement stores. Craft
foam shells can be found at craft stores.

Costume by Trulee Grace Hall

1. Find several different kinds of
green fabrics that remind you of
mermaids. You can use inexpensive
fabric remnants from a fabric store
or cut up old clothing that you no
longer use. Cut a fish-scale shape
from each of the fabrics (long, flat
on one side, curved on the other).
Use your first scale as a template to
create others. Depending on your
size, you may need several dozen
scales in each fabric. This is a great
project to do while you're doing
something else like talking on the
phone or watching TV.

2. For the base, use a skirt that's a
thrift store find or cast-off in a
green or shimmery aqua-colored
fabric. Since you won't see much of
the skirt under the scales, it's OK if
it's damaged. The skirt should be

tight fitting, preferably made of a
stretchy synthetic material, and
should reach to mid-calve length.
Lay the skirt on a flat surface and,
starting at the waistband, hot glue
the scales to the skirt (you can sew
them on if you know how). Layer
the scales like roof shingles so that
very little of the original skirt shows
through. When you get to the bottom of the skirt, let the scales hang
over the edge a little as a fringe.

3. The tail (made from the athletic
shorts) will flair out from underneath the skirt. You can cut open
the outside of the shorts so that the
material drags enough to hide your
feet, and cut open the inside so that
your legs are hidden The shorts
should appear to split in the middle
and come to two points at your feet.
Stretch out the elastic waist of the
shorts and hot glue the top of shorts
to the bottom edge of the skirt so
that the overlapping scales hide the
top. You should only apply the glue
in a few places rather than all
around so that the shorts will drape
more loosely around your ankles.

4. Hot glue sequin trim to the top
of the skirt at the waistband to dis-
tinguish your human half from your
fish tail. You can also add it on the
bottom of the tail.

5. For your human half, use a tank
top, slip, or even a long-sleeved
green shirt that can be tucked inside
the skirt. Hot glue two thin wooden
shell shapes or craft foam shells to
the shirt in the appropriate place.

6. Shell jewelry or faux pearls with
shells glued on and draped around
your neck will add the finishing
touches. Wear flip-flops, green socks,
or no shoes at all.

Dynamic Duos

You don't have to go it alone with your creative costume concept on Halloween. Get your party companion to join you in a couples' costume for double the impact. There are plenty of dynamic duos to choose from, real or imaginary, famous or infamous—dozens of ideas will spring to mind once you start to think about it.

We've come up with a couple of couples (pardon the pun) that we think will raise eyebrows and elicit admiring comments from your fellow partygoers. If your party posse includes more than two, you can also go as a terrific three-some or glorious group.

Queen Bee & Drone

Looking for a sure-fire way to create a buzz at any Halloween party? Find a willing drone and go as the Queen Bee. Here's a quick review of beehive politics: the queen bee has thousands of drones at her disposal, flying around and collecting nectar as she sits regally on her throne back at the hive laying thousands of eggs. The young, willing drones live only to mate with the queen and then die immediately after doing so. This is the perfect costume to wear if you're commitment-shy and want to get the message across to your date.

YOU WILL NEED

Yellow electrical tape

Black clothing
for top and bottom

Scissors

Black deer netting

Black stretch belt

Stapler and staples

Black spray paint

Aluminum flashing

Ballpoint pen

Metal repair tape or duct tape

Landscape fabric

Needle and thread

Polyester fiberfill

Safety pins

Costume by Joan Morris
Drone's Wings by Diana Light

Both the queen and the drone will tape strips of yellow electrical tape to their clothing. The queen looks best in a leotard with tights underneath, while the drone can get away with wearing a black turtleneck or sweatshirt and some jeans (he is a worker, after all). The drone then needs only to add a tool belt, some boots, and some sort of antennae—this one is a fur-covered headband with a black pipe cleaner wrapped around it. For the insect wings, see instructions on page 23.

The queen's costume is a little more detailed. For the skirt, cut deer netting to the desired length, then staple it to a black belt. We added several layers, pleated for fullness. You can spray paint the staples black to hide them.

The crown is made from aluminum flashing, which you'll fit to your head. Just draw a honeycomb pattern on the flashing with a pen or marker and cut out the center inside the pattern. Tape the crown closed at the back with metal repair tape or duct tape.

To make the stinger, cut two triangular pieces of the landscape fabric. Sew or staple the pieces together wrong side out, leaving a small opening so that you can stuff the stinger. Turn it right side out and stuff it with fiberfill, then fold over the open edges and safety pin them in place. Staple the stinger to the top of the belt.

Mr. & Mrs. Frank N. Stein

If Frankenstein's monster and his mate were created today, they wouldn't be caught undead in anything but duct tape clothing. A few years back, underground fashionistas started making wallets and handbags from duct tape, and the trend quickly spread. Soon high school students were making all kinds of clothing from this humble but durable material. Duct tape clothing has become all the rage at prom time thanks to a national contest with big cash prizes sponsored by a prominent duct tape company.

Designer Casey Browning (also a high school student) created these amazing duct tape fashions. If you're going to join the duct tape revolution on Halloween, remember that this is not lightweight, airy material, so you'll be dragging around a few extra pounds. Also, duct tape doesn't "breathe" like so many modern fabrics, so things could get a bit slippery inside your costume.

YOU WILL NEED

Duct tape

Scissors

Cardboard (optional)

Upholstery foam

Fishing line or clear thread

Large-eye needle

Gray paint

Small paintbrush

Clear elastic cord

Costume by Casey Browning

FOR THE DRESS

1. Start with a strip of duct tape that runs from your shoulder to ankle (or whatever length you want the dress to be). Place the strip (adhesive side up) on the floor, and cut another piece of the same length. Line up the outside edges of the two pieces and press the adhesive side of each together. This forms a strip with two smooth sides and no sticky mess.

2. Take another strip of the same length and lay one-third of this piece over the first piece. Then back this with a fourth piece of the same length.

3. Continue the process of overlapping and backing until the strips form a sheet of duct tape that is big enough to go from one side of you to the other. Repeat the same process to build the back half of the dress.

4. When you've built both sides of the dress, cut the two panels into the shape you want (curved in above the hips, flared at the bottom, etc.).

5. To join the two panels, just line up the sides and position a piece of duct tape (sticky side down) overlapping each panel. Repeat this process until the sides are joined, then repeat it on the other side.

6. To add the sleeves, build two panels just like the ones you built to make the front and back of the dress. Wrap one of the panels around your arm and tape it together to fit, then repeat this process for the other sleeve.

7. To attach the sleeves to the dress, cut holes in the top of the sleeves and corresponding holes in the shoulders of the dress. Lace the sleeves to the dress with a thin strip of duct tape.

8. Cut a slit down one of the sides from the underarm almost to the bottom of the dress. Put a strip of hook-and-loop fastener tape on each side inside the slit. Now you can get in and out of the dress.

9. For the neck detail, cut a slit from the neck down to about 4 inches (10.2 cm) above the waist. Cut equally spaced holes on each side of the slit. For the lacing, take a long piece of duct tape and fold it in half so that the sticky side folds back on itself. Lace this strip up through the holes.

10. To make the collar, cut a cardboard rectangle with a flared top, and cover it (front and back) with duct tape. Tape the collar to the outside of the neck.

FOR THE NECK BOLTS

1. Cut two pieces of upholstery foam into 1 x 2-inch (2.5 x 5.1 cm) cylinders.

2. Cut two more pieces into hexagon shapes, each with a 1-inch (2.5 cm) diameter. Each hexagon should be about $\frac{1}{2}$-inch (1.3 cm) thick.

3. Sew the hexagon to the cylinder with a large-eyed needle and piece of fishing line.

4. Wrap fishing line around the cylinder to squeeze it into a bolt shape. Paint the whole piece gray and let dry.

5. Poke a hole through the end of each bolt with the needle and thread a piece of elastic through the hole. Fit the bolts to your neck and tie the elastic in back when you've got the right fit.

FOR THE JACKET

Follow the same overlapping process you used to make the dress, except that the sleeves are attached directly to the jacket.

MOTHER NATURE & THE GREEN MAN

Peeking out of the leaves in the forest are two mysterious figures swathed in green. Are they human, supernatural, or a little bit of both? This costumed couple consists of Mother Nature, the all-powerful source of life on earth, and the Green Man (see page 38 for much more info), the enigmatic medieval archetype of the woods whose leafy face is fascinating but a little frightening. If you and your party companion are friends of the earth, this is the most enviro-friendly couples' costume you can create.

What's the fuzzy green stuff they're both wearing? It's a natural fiber material designed to line the bottom of hanging baskets and flowerbeds to encourage growth and keep out weeds. It looks fantastic and is the perfect material for this costume, but we won't lie to you—it's itchy and it sheds. You *must* wear something under your costume if you use it, and you'll definitely have to vacuum your floor later (it's best to assemble this in the garage or basement). This is one of those one-night-only materials. The good news is that as you prepare your garden for next spring, you need only lay your costume down in the soil and let Mother Nature work her magic. If you can't find this marvelous material, try using green felt instead or dye a piece of white faux fur green.

Costumes by Joan Morris
Leaf mask by Terry Taylor

MOTHER NATURE

Mother Nature wears a green shirt that's been embellished with an array of fake natural elements—silk flowers, leaves, vines, and butterflies; stuffed birds; and plastic berries. All the greenery is cut from craft store finds and hot glued to the shirt. The birds come with wires attached to their legs, so the wires were poked through the shirt and twisted shut.

The skirt is simply two pieces of fiber basket liner cut in a flared-skirt shape. To attach the pieces, we poked holes along the sides of each piece with an awl and laced the sides together with leather cord, knotting it at the bottom. We cut a few slits along the top to thread an adjustable belt through. More vines, birds, and leaves grace Mother Nature's skirt, kept in place with hot glue.

Now for the *pièce de résistance*—the hat. The base is simply an old hat from a thrift store. We hot glued silk leaves over it to cover it up, then hot glued the nest on top (you can find these nests at any craft store). Add birds (cardinals are nice and colorful), bird's eggs, and silk flowers to make it more inviting. Wildlife of all kinds will flock to Mother Nature in this comely costume.

THE GREEN MAN

The Green Man's tunic is also made from fiber liner—one long strip folded in half, with a circle cut out at the fold line for the neck hole. Holes for lacing were poked in sides on both the front and back with an awl. Leather cord is laced through the holes to stitch the front and back together, and knotted at the end. A front slit with leather lacing was added at the front for a little more comfort and interest.

The Green Man wears fake vines and oak leaves as well as real birch bark, all attached with hot glue. This modern green man (who's a gardener in real life) wears jeans under his tunic, but any casual pants would be acceptable.

The Green Man's crowing glory is the oak leaf mask, which should be left on at all times! Whatever you do, don't try to make this mask from the fiber liner material. Use craft foam as a base instead. Trace a basic mask shape (page 99) onto a piece of brown or green craft foam. Extend the shape below the eyes down to rest on the cheek, leaving the nose and mouth uncovered. Punch holes on both sides of the mask, level with the eye holes. Hot glue real or artificial leaves (oak leaves look best) to the mask, overlapping them as desired. Thread a doubled length of cord or ribbon through the holes.

WHO IS THE GREEN MAN?

*A*midst the dizzying spires and ornamental arches of many Medieval churches, a careful observer may often discover a curious face: the man's penetrating eyes stare out from behind a mask of leaves as vines spew from his mouth, nose, and ears, and branches sprout from his head. In a moment, it seems, the twisting, thriving vegetation will consume his face entirely and the human will disappear from sight, leaving only a tangle of greenery. Out of place among the pious statues of saints and serene Madonnas, this figure elicits curiosity. Who is the man with the leafy face? For lack of an explanation, modern scholars have taken to calling him the "Green Man."

The Green Man has puzzled historians for centuries. He seems a peculiarly pagan image to find in churches, but that's just where he started to appear starting around the thirteenth century, long after Christianity had taken root in Europe. The face behind the *masque feuillu* or mask of leaves was not a new image in the Middle Ages. Many believe the image comes from the Celts and their horned god of the forest, Cernunnos. Across Europe, the "wild man," a giant figure

Ceramic art by Christopher Mello

who wears a suit of leaves, is a familiar part of folk traditions and festivals. The English have a character called "Jack of the Wood" or "Jack of the Green" who walks through the streets on May Day wearing a crown of garlands and a wooden frame covered in foliage. Are these figures incarnations of the Green Man?

The sheer variety of interpretations of the Green Man is compelling. His face is sometimes frightening, sometimes sad, sometimes comic, and sometimes afraid. It is sometimes made of oak leaves, other times hawthorn, and later, during the Renaissance, composed occasionally of fruit and vegetables. His image seems to have been rendered mostly by stone masons or woodcarvers and is rarely seen in paintings or illuminated manuscripts. The vast majority of Green Man images that have survived until today are in or on churches, with the occasional one showing up in a private home or shop (this may be because virtually no other buildings from the time remain standing). It's not always easy to find a Green Man image in a church—they're often tucked in secret places and seem to jump out at people. Across the board, however, one constant remains true about Green Man imagery. There is a sense that the greenery that engulfs him is still growing and that he is very much alive.

What does the image of the Green Man mean? There are many theories. The wildness of nature was a fact of life for medieval people. For them, the forest was not a benevolent retreat, but a frightening place, fraught with danger. A face peeking from behind a tree could be a potential attacker and was not necessarily human. Forest spirits and fairies didn't have the pleasant reputation they have today. They were mischievous, sometimes even devilish, capable of stealing babies and eating them. Some speculate the Green Man represented a forest

demon and appeared on churches to threaten believers and dissuade them from sinful behavior. Taking a more positive view, some say he represents God in nature. Another theory is more mundane—perhaps the Green Man didn't have much significance and was just part of the repertoire of architectural motifs of the day, no different from angels, mermaids, or dragons.

Despite contemporary speculation, no one can really say with certainty how his medieval creators viewed the Green Man. The truth about his meaning was lost at the end of the Middle Ages. Modern-day environmentalists see him as the symbol of our connection to the natural world. Pub owners and beer brewers use his leafy visage on pub signs and bottle labels. Whatever his meaning or his origin, this intriguing figure continues to confound and captivate those who are lucky enough to encounter him.

Party Arty

If the muse hasn't visited you with a whole host of fabulous costume ideas yet, try plugging into a theme. Peruse your art history books and come up with a costume based on a work of art. If you're hosting a Halloween gathering, an art party is a great theme.

Keep the Fauves away from the Impressionists.

MONET'S WATER LILIES

When you're going for instant recognition in your art costume, you can't make a much safer choice than Monet's water lilies. Even in the most boorish of company, you'd be hard-pressed to find someone who has reached adulthood without encountering one of Monet's many water lily paintings. They're popular for a reason (besides loose licensing agreements): they're peaceful and beautiful, and the costume that you make to represent them can be too.

For this interpretation, we found the perfect starting point: a vintage dress of deep purple fabric with a shimmering aqua blue organza overlay. Any clothing in blue, green, or watery-looking tones would do. The lily pads that float over the dress are from aquarium and pond supply stores. They're sewn to the dress with a few simple loops of invisible thread. To accessorize the dress, we added a choker and wrist corsage, each made from a piece of beautiful blue iridescent ribbon. The corsage and choker can be cut to fit and fastened in the back with hook-and-loop fastener tape.

The ultimate topper is the little pillbox hat, which is a thrift store find re-covered with the ribbon used for the corsage and choker. Atop the hat sits a ceramic water lily and a little ceramic bridge, reminiscent of the bridge at Giverny seen in many of the water lily paintings. This bridge was made for use in bonsai gardens; you can find miniature bridges made for fish tanks, too. Yes, the bridge is smaller than the giant water lily in front of it. It's called *perspective*.

POLLOCK PAINTING

During his lifetime, Jackson Pollock was often misunderstood. Looking at his giant canvases covered in free-form paint splatters, his detractors would often say, "Anyone could do that!" Here's your chance to prove the critics right (or wrong as the case may be). Pollock is a great choice for an art party costume because his trademark spontaneous pouring technique is so well-known and was so often imitated. While your own efforts may not come close to Pollock's masterpieces, you'll at least have a chance to go nuts with a few cans of paint.

YOU WILL NEED

LARGE PIECE OF UNPRIMED CANVAS
LATEX PAINTS IN SEVERAL COLORS*
PAINTBRUSHES, WOODEN SPOONS,
OR STIRRING STICKS
TARP OR NEWSPAPER
HOT GLUE GUN AND GLUE STICKS

*Latex dries faster and is easier to clean up than other paints.

Costume by Trulee Grace Hall

1. Measure and cut a piece of unprimed canvas that will reach from the front of your knees, over your shoulders, and down to the back of your knees. Use whatever width suits the painting you want to be, whether it's a horizontal or vertical piece. The canvas will be more comfortable to wear if it doesn't extend too far past your shoulders.

2. Fold the canvas in half lengthwise and cut a hole in the middle big enough for your head.

3. Now comes the fun part. You will most certainly make a mess, so work outside or use a tarp or a lot of newspaper under the canvas. Spread out your canvas so that it is completely flat. Refer to a favorite Pollock painting when picking your colors, or use what you have. Use paintbrushes, sticks, and spoons to aggressively and generously

splatter, drip, splash, and attack the canvas with paint! Have fun with this—don't be timid. Let the paint splatter off the sides of the canvas.

4. Let the canvas dry completely. It will take at least a day and a half to two days, though it will dry faster in the sun.

5. Once dry, hot glue the sides of the canvas together, leaving plenty of room for your arms to move about freely. Wear your Pollock canvas over all black, and since he was a contemporary of the Beatniks, a black beret is a nice touch. If you're so inclined, drink hi-balls, smoke, and spout off everything you know about abstract expressionism until you notice other partygoers avoiding you.

CALDER MOBILE HAT

Don't overlook sculptors when looking for inspiration for your art costume.
This cute, quirky hat is modeled after Alexander Calder's bold modern mobiles.
Research Calder mobiles and decide on colors and shapes for your wire structure.
Wear an all-black ensemble with your hat to resemble the big black legs on many of
his massive public works. If your fellow partygoers are unfamiliar with Calder,
just tell them you're a *kinetic sculpture*. They'll still be confused.

YOU WILL NEED

POSTER BOARD

SCISSORS

HEAVY PACKING TAPE OR DUCT TAPE

HOT GLUE AND GLUE STICKS

METAL SWIVEL CLASP

CRAFT FOAM IN SEVERAL COLORS

HEAVY-GAUGE WIRE

NEEDLE-NOSE PLIERS

Hat by Trulee Grace Hall

1. Fit a piece of poster board to your head and cut it into a small cone shape (see page 90 for more details). Cut a piece of craft foam to cover the triangle, trimming the edges as necessary. Hot glue the two pieces together. Use heavy packing tape or hot glue to secure the sides of the cone together. You could also just spray paint the cone black if you're pressed for time.

2. Find a little metal, swiveling clasp at a hardware store. There's an endless variety of little gadgets to choose from. Imagine something that might be at the end of a dog collar. At the point of the cone, cut a hole big enough to accommodate the swiveling end of the clasp. Hot glue it into place, being sure not to glue the swiveling parts, disabling the movement all together.

3. Refer to a Calder mobile as you start to cut the wires for your mobile. First, cut a central piece of wire that will extend up from the end of the metal clasp. Attach branches of wire off this central wire using the pliers to bend and wrap the wire into desired positions. To avoid frustration, keep your design simple. You may wish to hot glue the fragile connections in place.

4. Cut out several small shapes from your foam. For every shape, make two identical pieces. Sandwich each couple around the ends of the wire, and hot glue them together. You will need to experiment with weight and balance to make sure that your miniature mobile will not be lopsided. Bigger shapes are heavier, and longer wire adds weight as well. Be intuitive and have fun with it.

Botticelli's
Allegory of Spring

For our costume we started with a white dress from a thrift store, but you could also use an old summer nightgown or a white peasant shirt and loose, flowing white skirt. Simply choose an assortment of silk flowers and cut the stems off. Hot glue the flowers to the dress in a random arrangement, adding leaves under the flowers where it suits you. Be careful! Using hot glue on this scale can lead to burns. Try wearing gloves during this process. Choose some silk or plastic flower garland and hot glue it to the waist and neckline of your dress or nightgown.

Some would say that to be called "Botticellian" is one of the highest compliments a woman can receive. All the women in Botticelli's paintings are ethereally beautiful. Think of Venus in the *Birth of Venus*, her blonde tresses cascading and her sweet expression. If you really want to make an impression on Halloween you could go as her, replete with half shell.

Remember, though, she is wearing nothing but her famed blonde tresses. If you're slightly more demure, you could be *la Primavera* (also called Flora, the goddess of flowers), the allegory of spring in Botticelli's *second* most famous painting. You'll be a breath of fresh air on a chilly fall evening, and it's probably one of the most flattering costume choices you could make.

You'll need a flower garland head-piece. This one is made in the same way as the autumn garland on page 94, except that we used spring flowers and greenery. An organdy ribbon down the back is a nice touch.

To embody the spirit of Flora, carry a basket of flowers (real or fake) and scatter them about at will. Sprinkle Italian phrases into your conversation and make sure to kiss everyone on both cheeks when you greet them.

Out of the (Linen) Closet

Your closet may indeed harbor skeletons on Halloween, but it also plays host to a treasure trove of costume materials. Sift through the piles of laundry and linens for abandoned sheets, tablecloths, napkins, and curtains to fold, cut, and convert into costumes that transcend the classic bed sheet ghost. Kimonos, robes, wrap skirts, and headpieces are just a few ideas to inspire you.

HERE COMES *the* JUDGE

If you never get a chance to pass judgment on people during your daily life, Halloween offers the opportunity. In your judge persona, you can make up creative sentencing for people who wear bad costumes or take the last chocolate chip cookie from the dessert table. If you really want to intimidate people, carry a noose and be a hanging judge. Then again, how intimidating can you really be with a bunch of toilet paper rolls on your head?

JUDGE'S ROBE

The robe is simply a red bed sheet, double-sized. You could also use a big tablecloth or curtain. Simply wrap the sheet around you and discreetly tuck one end under the other. You can safety pin it together if you like.

JUDGE'S WIG

You don't need to start collecting empty paper towel or toilet paper months in advance to make the headpiece. Sending out an e-mail at work should immediately net you dozens of rolls from eco-conscious coworkers who recycle. If you use paper towel rolls, just cut them in half and sand the rough edges a bit.

When you've got enough rolls to make about five long plaits (the four side plaits on this wig used 11 rolls, while the top and center plait used 17), paint them white with craft or spray paint.

To sew your wig together, double thread a large-eye needle with fishing line. Poke a hole through one side of one roll, and pull the needle through to the other side with small pliers. Make a knot and cover it with a drop of cyanoacrylate glue to make sure the line doesn't slip back through the hole. Add another roll to the same piece of fishing line using the same process. Keep going until your plait reaches the length you want. Repeat the threading process on the opposite end of the roll to make it sturdy. After you've got four plaits of equal length, make one that's long enough to go across the top of your head and match the length of the side plaits.

Lay all your plaits on a flat surface with the longer one in the middle. Sew the plaits together, securing each one to the long center plait and adding one loop on the top roll that ties each plait to the one adjacent to it.

NECK *&* WRIST RUFFLES

For the Neck Ruffle

Lay two large coffee filters on top of each other and fold them into a triangle. Repeat for two more sets of coffee filters for a total of three sets of two-layer triangles. Staple the top of the triangles so that the folds stay down.

Center one of the triangles on top of another and staple the two together. Make sure you only staple through the first layer rather than all the way through—that way the staples will be hidden. Center the joined triangles on top of the third triangle and staple, again hiding staples. You'll have a staggered look.

Center a piece of ribbon near the top of the top triangle. Fold the point of the triangle over and staple to create a flap. Tie the ribbon around your neck to wear the ruffle. On the front side of the ruffles (the side where you can't see staples), punch holes around the edges of the coffee filters to create a lacey look.

For the Cuffs

Slit four coffee filters on one side and cut the flat center out of them. Stack them on top of each other. Staple white ribbon around the open edge. You can paint over the staples with correction liquid if you want to.

Punch holes around the edges for the lace effect. Repeat the whole process for the second cuff.

Wig by Diana Light
Cuffs by Joan Morris

BED SHEET GEISHA

You may have seen someone wearing a geisha costume before. Chances are she was wearing a bathrobe. The problem with this costume solution is that instead of looking like you're about to entertain gentlemen in a teahouse, you look as though you're about to brush your teeth and go to bed. Try making a kimono from a sheet instead. You don't need to sew it together, although you can if you know how. Add a geisha mask made from a clip art image (it can serve as a fan, too).

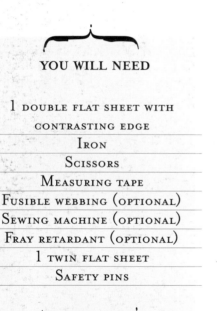

YOU WILL NEED

1 DOUBLE FLAT SHEET WITH
CONTRASTING EDGE

IRON

SCISSORS

MEASURING TAPE

FUSIBLE WEBBING (OPTIONAL)

SEWING MACHINE (OPTIONAL)

FRAY RETARDANT (OPTIONAL)

1 TWIN FLAT SHEET

SAFETY PINS

Costume by Joan Morris

FOR THE KIMONO

1. Iron the sheet, then cut off the contrasting edge and set it aside until later.

2. Fold the sheet in half. Locate the center of the fold with a measuring tape and mark the center. Cut out a neck hole at this spot, then cut down the length of the sheet. This will be the front opening of the kimono.

3. Measure 12 inches (30.5 cm) in from each short side of the sheet and cut in a straight line from the edge to this line. Measure 26 inches (66 cm) down from the fold and cut in so that your cut ends at the 12-inch (30.5 cm) mark, cutting off the bottom of the sheet so that you have sleeves.

4. Close up the side seams of the sleeves with the fusible webbing and an iron or the sewing machine.

5. Reattach the contrasting edge over the front opening and neck hole, either with the fusible webbing or sewing machine. It doesn't have to reach the end of the kimono, just to about your knee.

FOR THE OBI

Fold the twin flat sheet lengthwise into a 12-inch (30.5 cm) wide strip and safety pin the edges together. Tie the obi around the back.

Mask instructions on page 98.

FETCHING FLAMENCA

If you'd rather be alluring than alarming this Halloween, you can't go wrong with a flamenca costume. Delve into the depths of your linen drawer and find an old red tablecloth, or pick one up at a thrift store. Wear a black leotard on top, and if your own hair won't cooperate, add a black wig so your mantilla will have a secure place to sit. A fan is a must-have accessory for flirting provocatively with your admirers. Be prepared to perform Spanish dances on demand.

YOU WILL NEED

OLD RED TABLECLOTH, CURTAIN, FABRIC SCRAP, OR LARGE SCARF

SCISSORS

RED AND BLACK CREPE PAPER

HOT GLUE GUN AND GLUE STICKS

LACE OR DOILY

BLACK SPRAY PAINT

PLASTIC FOOD CONTAINER OR TRANSPARENT PLASTIC SHEET

HAIR COMB

BLACK TULLE

Costume by Emma Pearson

1. Wrap the tablecloth or fabric around yourself to make sure it fits. You don't want it to be too tight, as you'll need a little extra fabric for the tie of the skirt. The back should be slightly longer than the front with the longest point in the middle of the back of the skirt.

2. Cut the material into a half circle with two tabs for the ties on the flat edge. Make two small holes in the tabs. You will thread each tab through the hole in the opposite tab to tie the skirt closed.

3. The next step is best done outdoors. Lay the skirt out on a flat surface and lay the lace or doily over it. Spray paint over the lace with black spray paint to create a stenciled lace effect on the red fabric.

4. Glue the first layer of crepe paper around the bottom edge of the skirt with a glue gun, adding two additional layers in contrasting colors as the previous layer dries. Glue only the inner edge of the paper so that the outer edge remains loose to resemble lace.

5. Create the crepe paper sleeve ruffles the same way you made the skirt ruffle—just use short pieces of crepe paper sized to fit your shoulders. You can just tape the ruffles to your shoulders rather than gluing them down so that you can use the leotard later for something else.

6. For the mantilla, cut a rectangle with a slightly flared top from the transparent plastic. The bottom of the rectangle should be the same width as the hair comb.

7. Place the lace or doily over the transparent plastic rectangle and spray paint over it with black spray paint. The lace pattern will be stenciled onto the plastic.

8. Hot glue the transparent piece onto the comb.

9. Hot glue a black tulle veil to the back of the comb and arrange the comb in your hair or wig.

FORMERLY FORMAL

It all begins with a promise. He and she promise to love each other forever. She promises you, her best friend, will be right there beside her as she takes her vows. Then she promises that you will be able to wear that dress again.

Yes, that peach-colored, puffy-sleeved, taffeta dress that makes you look like a circus attraction. You can wear it again, but *only* as a Halloween costume. First, embrace the fact that there is absolutely nothing you can do to make this dress wearable, except as a costume. Once you've come to terms with that, you will be free to disassemble it and reinterpret it in any way you can dream up.

BEFORE

Three classic bridesmaid or formal styles: the puffy-sleeved with a ribbon in back, the spaghetti strap with an a-line skirt (okay, this one really isn't all that bad) and the empire waist, short puffy sleeves with a draping neckline.

AFTER

It took less than three hours to transform each of these dresses, and none of them required sewing. Turn the page to find out how each dress was reinterpreted.

DRESS I

What a difference a spray makes! This dress went from classic 1980s bridal to Queen Elizabeth I. The waistline suggested an Elizabethan style, so the bow was removed and the back became the front. A generous coat of metallic gold spray paint over the entire dress made things better immediately. Upholstery remnants were used for the panels. The pattern on the middle panel and the sleeve additions was made by laying a piece of lace over the top of the fabric and spray painting through it. The sleeves were secured inside the puffs with electrical tape. The stripes on the puffy sleeves were attached with hot glue, as was the fabric panel over the top center. Those little gold crosses are flooring tile spacers spray painted gold. Little faux pearls are hot glued to the center. A little inexpensive trim was hot glued along the edges. Finally, we spray painted doilies and taped them inside the sleeves and under the waistline to resemble lace. Add some faux pearls, and you're ready to start crushing the Spanish Armada.

DRESS II

Something about the silver of this dress said Marie Antoinette. This design was based very loosely on one of her later portraits. She liked layers and lots of ribbons. The fabric sashes were attached to the dress by poking a thin wire through the dress and twisting it on the inside (you could also sew them on with invisible thread). A ribbon is tied over the wire to hide it. If you're worried about the sashes staying in place, pull the wire as tightly as you can to secure it. The panel on the top is just attached with hot glue, as is the ribbon trim. That's all there is to it. If you'd like to be more authentic cut the sleeves of a poofy blouse and attach them to the spaghetti straps with hot glue. Add big ribbons at the elbow, and you'll be almost authentic. To achieve the look of *panniers* (the puffs at the hips) stuff clothing or pillows under the skirt and secure them in place with wire tied under the waistband.

DRESS III

This is the 20-minute costume solution. The shape of this dress said 1830, so it was transformed into a sleek gown for the Voodoo Queen, Marie Laveau (see page 149). First, a generous coat of blood-red spray paint was applied to the entire dress, except for the belt, which was spray painted black. A black fringe was hot glued near the bottom of the dress. Black tulle was stuffed into the sleeve openings and neckline to finish it off. Add a black headwrap and some large hoop earrings, and you'll enchant all who see you.

BASIC BLACK *&* OTHER WITCHWEAR

What would a witch (or warlock) wear? Your very own wardrobe may be the perfect place to start assembling a spooky or spectacular look for Halloween. Under ordinary circumstances, that black turtleneck you wear to work once a week may seem perfectly respectable, and even downright dull, but pair it with some black leggings, a pair of wings or spider legs, or a beak and it becomes the start of something sensational.

Before you go out and invest in costume materials, look deep into your own closet, keeping an eye out for simple shapes and lines, or interesting flourishes. Consider anything that you haven't worn in years a candidate for ripping, tearing, and cutting into a new costume-worthy shape. With a little imagination, a neglected and long-forgotten skirt becomes the basis of a mermaid tail (see page 28) and an old pair of pointy-toed shoes polish off a witch's ensemble. Your costume jewelry may seem to gaudy for everday, but it's perfect for Halloween when excess is the rule of the day.

A swim cap makes your hair disappear, leaving your head open for reinterpretation in any number of ways. Tights, when stretched over wire, can be fashioned into wings, and socks, when stuffed with cotton or fiberfill, look an awful lot like ears. Solid colored clothing of any kind in black, white, red, or green serves as the perfect backdrop for any costume that's witchy, devilish, mystical, or earthy. Remember the advice your mother gave you before heading out into the winter cold, and layer, layer, layer.

LAUNDRY LIST OF COSTUME BASICS

LONG OR SHORT BLACK GLOVES

TIGHTS IN BLACK, GREEN, BROWN, WHITE, OR STRIPES

SCARVES

STRETCHY RUNNING PANTS OR TOPS

STRETCHY BICYCLE SHORTS

LONG BLACK OR WHITE SKIRT

SHORT BLACK OR WHITE SKIRT

BLACK TURTLENECK, LONG-SLEEVED SHIRT OR LEOTARD

WHITE TURTLENECK, LONG-SLEEVED SHIRT, OR LEOTARD

CAPES OF ANY KIND

SWIM CAPS OR TIGHT-FITTING CAPS OF ANY KIND

ANY CLOTHING WITH INTERESTING TEXTURE, SUCH AS FAUX FUR

CRINOLINE OR ANY OTHER FORMAL-WEAR FOUNDATION GARMENT

OLD NIGHTGOWN OR SLIP

OLD UNFASHIONABLE BOOTS (THEY'RE SPRAYPAINT-ABLE!)

POINTY SHOES

UNFASHIONABLE, OVERSIZED MEN'S SUITS

COSTUME JEWELRY

OLD HATS THAT CAN BE PAINTED, CUT, OR OTHERWISE TRANSFORMED

The Beast in You

Take a walk on the wild side on Halloween. Be a beast or a cuddly critter, or even a half-human, half-beast hybrid. Start with basic black pieces or cast-offs from your own wardrobe. Add appendages or protuberances to your human frame to become a creature that's fascinating, frightening, bewitching, or bewildering. In the following section, there are plenty of ideas to spark your imagination. The materials are inexpensive and easy to find if you don't already have them. The processes used to make the costumes are easy to learn, and almost none of them involve sewing!

LITTLE BIG HORNS

Horns on Halloween have a seemingly endless range of applications. Mythical creatures like centaurs, minotaurs, satyrs, and devils all have horns, not to mention real horned animals like rhinos. What's your sign? If you're an Aries, Capricorn, or Taurus, you can show it by donning a pair of these lightweight but lifelike horns. They're made from upholstery foam and transformed with a piece of string, wire, and a miracle product called patching cement. You can use this process to make hooves (see page 67), tusks (see page 68), or antlers, too.

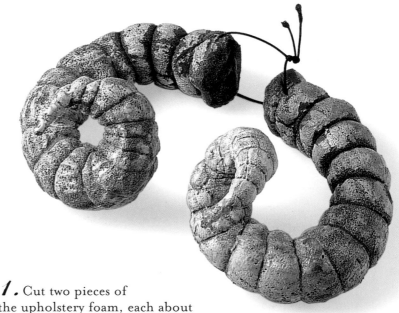

1. Cut two pieces of the upholstery foam, each about 1¼-feet (38.1 cm) long and about 2 inches (5.1 cm) wide (see figure 1). You can make the horns longer or wider depending on the size of your head and the type of horn you're making.

2. Round off both ends of the foam pieces.

3. Taper one end of each foam piece approximately 6 inches (15.2 cm) from the end. You will now have two matching cone-shaped pieces of foam (see figure 2).

4. Insert a piece of wire lengthwise through the center of each cone. Leave about 3 inches (7.6 cm) of wire sticking out of the wide bottom of each cone.

YOU WILL NEED

SCISSORS
UPHOLSTERY FOAM*
18-GAUGE FLEXIBLE STEEL WIRE
WHITE THREAD
WHITE ACRYLIC PATCHING CEMENT**
WHITE ACRYLIC PAINT
PAINTBRUSH
CLEAR ACRYLIC SEALER (SPRAY CAN)
LARGE-EYE NEEDLE
ELASTIC CORD

*Available at fabric stores
**Used for patching roofs. Available at hardware stores.

Horns by Shaina Heller

5. Bend the wire to form the cones into the shape you want.

6. Starting at the wide end of one cone, wrap thread tightly around the foam, forming jointed sections. Continue until you reach the tip of the cone (see figure 4). Repeat with the second cone, trying to keep your wrapping pattern as similar to the first horn as possible.

7. Bend the wire extensions at the base of each horn into small hooks.

8. Mix one part white acrylic patching cement with two parts white acrylic paint. You can either paint the mixture on the horns with the paintbrush or dip the horns into the mixture.

9. Hang the horns to dry. If you dipped the horns, make sure there are no clumps of the paint mixture left on them.

10. Paint the horns with the white acrylic paint and hang them to dry a second time.

11. Spray clear acrylic sealer over the horns and allow them to dry.

12. Use the needle to poke large holes in the inside top of each horn. Thread elastic cord through the hole and stretch it around your head to figure out how out long it should be to hold the horns snugly to your head.

13. Once the horns are strung, position them on your head.

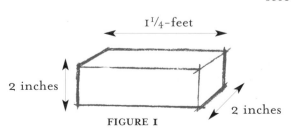

FIGURE 1

FIGURE 2

FIGURE 3

FIGURE 4

FROM THE NAIL FILE

French tips are out for Halloween this year—talons are in. If you're going to be a bloodthirsty vampira, a hideous man-eating harpy, or simply a bird of prey, you'll need to let your fingers do the talking. Transform your delicate digits into razor-sharp claws with this deceptively easy trick. The nails are made of foam from a vegetable packing tray, so they're lightweight, a little bit flexible, and won't draw blood when you run them across someone's arm.

Talons are always in fashion!

YOU WILL NEED

SCISSORS
FOAM VEGETABLE PACKING TRAY
OLD PAIR OF BLACK GLOVES
NEEDLE AND THREAD

Gloves by Lois Simbach

1. Cut out long fingernail shapes from the foam vegetable packing tray. You might want to cut out more than 10 in case one breaks when you are attaching them to the gloves.

2. Put on one of the gloves and carefully sew on the talons on with a contrasting color thread.

3. Repeat for the other glove. Don't try to paint the foam or glue it on with cement adhesive—it will bubble and dissolve.

THE RIGHT FOOT

Once you've decided to be a beast on Halloween, you've got to go all the way with your costume, from your head right down to your feet. Camouflage your all-too-human appendages with a pair of clawed feet. You can slip these on right over your work shoes so you get the dramatic look without the discomfort. You'll probably still be wearing them at the end of the night!

YOU WILL NEED

THIN CARDBOARD (ABOUT THE THICKNESS OF A CEREAL BOX)

MARKER OR PENCIL

SCISSORS

BLACK FABRIC

SPRAY ADHESIVE

ELASTIC OR NYLON BAND

HOT GLUE AND GLUE STICKS OR HEAVY-DUTY GLUE

HOOK-AND-LOOP FASTENER TAPE

Feet by Trulee Grace Hall

1. First, look at pictures of birds' feet to figure out what shape you want your feet to be. You may or may not want to curve the claws, for instance. Draw the shape you want onto a piece of cardboard. As you work on your design, hold the cardboard up to your own feet to be sure that your foot design is in correct proportion to your body. When you're satisfied with the way the foot looks, cut it out. Use the first foot as a template to cut out the second.

2. Bend the cardboard to make the claws three-dimensional. The top of the cardboard foot will rest on top of your shoe, and the claws will bend around its sides. Make sure that the claws are not so long that they will drag on the ground.

3. Cover the feet with the fabric of your choice. Place the foot on top of a square of fabric and cut around the shape, leaving a 1-inch (2.5 cm) border all around. Apply spray adhesive to the back of the fabric and press it onto the foot, tucking the borders underneath the contoured claws.

4. Place the foot on top of your shoe and measure out how much elastic you'll need to create a strap that goes around your ankle. You could also substitute a length of hook-and-loop fastener tape. Hot glue a strap onto the back of each foot shape, making sure that you can still slide it comfortably over your shoe. If you wish, attach another "toe" to the back of your bird foot by hot gluing it to the strap in the appropriate position.

MONSTER MITTS

In monster movies, human hands can spontaneously sprout hair and contort themselves into hideous gnarled appendages In reality, you're probably going to have to use gloves to give your hands such a terrifying look. Transforming gloves into scary monster mitts requires a little alchemy, in the form of matches, so be careful. Dr. Frankenstein may have created his monster in a laboratory, but you'll want to work outdoors, as this is a messy process and requires ventilation. To maintain a good grip, don't add anything to the palm of the glove. Party monsters still need to handle food and beverages.

Mitts by Lois Simbach

YOU WILL NEED

OLD NEWSPAPERS AND MAGAZINES

ALUMINUM FOIL

WHITE STIFF PLASTIC BOTTLE, OLD MILK JUG, OR DISH DETERGENT BOTTLE

SCISSORS

CANDLE

MATCHES

WHITE OIL-BASED PAINT

MEDIUM AND SMALL PAINTBRUSHES

LARGE MUSLIN GARDEN GLOVES

POLYESTER FIBERFILL

BABY POWDER

FAUX FUR

CEMENT ADHESIVE

LATEX WALL PAINT

FINGERNAIL POLISH

MINERAL SPIRITS

PAPER TOWELS

1. Lay down a few layers of old newspapers and a layer of aluminum foil to prepare for the process.

2. Cut talons from the curved part of the white plastic bottle. You'll want them to be about 2 inches (5.2 cm) long.

3. Light the candle and heat the talons over the flame. While they're still hot, bend them into scary talon shapes. Don't worry if some soot gathers on the talons—you'll paint over them later.

4. Use white oil-based paint to paint one side of the talons and allow them to dry for about one hour on the tin foil, then paint the other side.

5. Rip pages from an old magazine and stuff them into the gloves.

6. Cut the fiberfill into a few dozen small pieces, about 1 inch (2.5 cm) in diameter or smaller. Cut three additional large pieces (about 3 inches [7.6 cm] in diameter) and set them aside. You'll use these pieces as applicators for the adhesive.

7. Cut the faux fur into about 50 small pieces, less than 1 inch (2.5 cm) in diameter.

8. Apply the cement adhesive to the top of the gloves using the larger pieces of foam as applicators. Don't put too much adhesive on the glove—you need a thin, even coat.

9. Apply adhesive cement to each small piece of fiberfill and let them dry for about five minutes. Once partially dry, stick the fiberfill pieces one-by-one onto the parts of the glove you have already covered with the cement adhesive. Make sure that you don't press too hard and accidentally stick the glove to itself. As you work, coat your hands periodically with baby powder to prevent the cement adhesive from sticking to them. Don't peel the adhesive directly off your hands because it will pull the skin off too.

10. Working over aluminum foil, coat the small pieces of the faux fur with the cement adhesive and allow them to partially dry.

11. Put another light coat of the cement adhesive on the gloves around the fiberfill pieces. Stick the faux fur pieces onto the gloves. It's okay if the fur and the foam overlap in places (this is a monster, after all).

12. Allow the gloves to dry completely, then paint the gloves with the latex wall paint.

13. Apply cement adhesive to the ends of the talons with a piece of fiberfill. Allow them to dry a little bit, then press them onto the tips of the gloves.

14. When you have glued on all the talons, paint them with two coats of the fingernail polish. You might even add some red fingernail polish on the gloves for make-believe blood. Remove the balled up magazines from the gloves and let them dry for a few hours.

15. Use the mineral spirits to clean up any paint that might have spilled and to wash your brushes.

CHIC BEAK

If you've decided to be a bird for Halloween, you'll need a superior beak to remain at the top of the bird pecking order. Depending on what kind of bird you want to be, you can shape your beak to look sinister, benign, or elegant. This beak is accessorized with a tight-fitting red swim cap and a white feather boa to create a vulture look.

YOU WILL NEED

CRAFT FOAM
HOT GLUE
WIRE
SCISSORS
AWL
FABRIC OF YOUR CHOICE
ELASTIC CORD

Beak by Trulee Grace Hall

1. Cut a triangle from craft foam and shape it into a cone big enough to cover your nose and mouth. Join the sides with hot glue. Cut and bend a piece of strong wire into the desired shape of your beak (straight, hooked, etc). Hot glue the wire to the outside bottom of the cone. Cut out two more triangles from craft foam to cover the wire (since craft foam is flexible, it will conform to the shape of the wire). Cover these triangles in fabric if you wish, and glue them into position onto the beak frame.

2. Attach elastic cord to each side of the cone with hot glue, making sure that the beak fits snugly on your face. Use an awl or other poking tool to create air holes in an inconspicuous place on the beak.

A fetching costume...   *Indeed.*

A BUG'S EYE VIEW, & ANTENNAE, TOO

**Here's a very simple way to look less human
and more like an insect.**

YOU WILL NEED

OLD SUNGLASSES
FORAL WIRE
WIRE
BLACK PIPE CLEANERS
BLACK PERMANENT MARKER

Antennae by Diana Light

1. Start with an old pair of sunglasses. Join a few pieces of floral wire together end on end until you have enough to go around the lens of the sunglasses, and straight up to form a fairly long antenna. Twist black pipe cleaners around the floral wire, leaving a little bit of uncovered floral wire on either end. Tuck one of the uncovered ends over the nose bridge of the sunglasses.

2. Now that the wire is anchored, wind it around the plastic frame of the sunglasses, attaching it to the frame with hot glue. When you've covered the whole frame, let the rest of the wire stick up as an antenna, then hot glue a feather to the remaining end of the wire. Repeat for the other eye. Use a marker to draw a mesh pattern over the lens of the glasses to make it look like an insect's "compound eye."

HAIRY LEGS

One of the interesting things about half-human, half-animal creatures is that it's usually the bottom half that's an animal. Whatever the reason for this may be, it certainly makes it easier to make a creature costume. To become a hairy-legged beast, you need only cover up your own legs (which may or may not already be hairy) with faux fur pants or chaps. This is a no-sew costume, so don't be intimidated. It's held together with strong safety pins (but you ought to wear something underneath just in case).

YOU WILL NEED

Scissors

Faux fur scraps

Large safety pins or needle and thread

Awl or other hole poker

Leather cord

Cotton cord or laundry line

Craft glue

Strong tape

Tail by Diana Light
Pants by Joan Morris
Hooves by Shaina Heller

1. Cut out four pieces of the faux fur, each long enough to reach from your hips to your ankles and as wide as the pants you usually wear plus 1 foot (30.5 cm) extra.

2. Put the right sides of the fabric together and pin the crotch, side seams, and inseam with the safety pins.

3. Turn the pants right side out.

4. Poke holes in the waist with the awl.

5. Thread the leather cord through the holes and tie the cord at the front of the pants.

FOR THE TAIL

Cut as many pieces of cord as you think you'll need for a substantial tail. Make your pieces twice as long as you want your tail to be, as you will be folding them in half. Dip the ends in clear-drying glue to prevent them from fraying. Fold the pieces of cord in half, then tape the bundle together with a narrow piece of duct tape or other strong tape. Hide the tape by hot gluing a few pieces of cord over it. Slide a large open safety pin into the bundle, attaching it to a few strands and leaving the open side facing out. Safety pin the tail to your wooly pants.

THUNDERING HOOVES

These lifelike hooves are a must-have accessory for any creature costume. They're made with an ingenious process that transforms ordinary upholstery foam (the stuff you put in pillows) into a stiff, yet still lightweight material that can be shaped and painted to resemble any kind of beastly body part, such as bones, horns (see page 58), or tusks (see page 68). These hooves are so comfortable to wear, you'll be the fastest-footed critter on the dance floor.

YOU WILL NEED

SHOES TO BE WORN WITH COSTUME
UPHOLSTERY FOAM*
MARKER
RULER
SCISSORS
WHITE ACRYLIC PATCHING CEMENT**
WHITE ACRYLIC PAINT
PAINT BRUSH
ACRYLIC PAINT, ANOTHER COLOR OF YOUR CHOICE
CLEAR SPRAY ACRYLIC SEALER
ELASTIC CORD
LARGE-EYED NEEDLE AND THREAD

*Available at fabric stores
**Available at hardware stores

Hooves by Shaina Heller

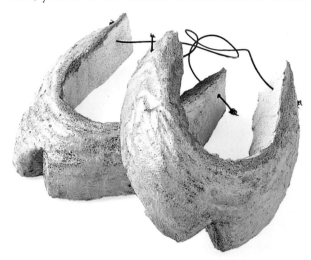

1. Place one of your shoes on top of a piece of foam and trace the front of the shoe with a marker.

2. Measure and trace a 1¹/₂-inch (1.3 cm) border around the outline of the shoe that you just traced (see figure 1).

3. Cut out the outer U-shaped curve that you have drawn on the foam, and repeat the process for your other shoe.

4. Taper the outside ends of the U-shape (see figure 2).

5. Cut out the center part of the U-shape.

6. Taper the shaded area.

7. Turn the first hoof upside down and taper it underneath leaving ¹/₂-inch (1.3 cm) of foam intact. Repeat the process for the other hoof.

8. Cut a ³/₄-inch (1.9 cm) "v" shape for the cleft in the center front of each hoof.

9. Mix one part white acrylic patching cement with two parts white acrylic paint.

10. Paint the hooves twice with the paint and patching cement mixture, letting them dry in between coats.

11. Paint the hooves with acrylic paint to achieve a bone-colored look.

12. Spray the clear acrylic sealer over the hooves and allow them to dry.

13. Attach elastic cord on the back of one of the hooves with the needle and the thread, then pull the cord around the back of your shoe and attach it to the other side of the hoof.

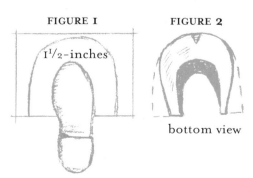

FIGURE 1

1¹/₂-inches

FIGURE 2

bottom view

THE WALRUS

Coo coo ca cho. You are the walrus. You could also be the egg man, or the elementary penguin, but does anyone really remember the rest of the lyrics to that song? Along with your walrus tusks, wear a tweedy suit and a bowler hat. You'll look as though you're sitting in an English garden waiting for the sun.

Tusks by Shaina Heller

YOU WILL NEED

Scissors

Upholstery foam

Aluminum foil

Plaster gauze

Paint brushes

Marker

Water

White craft glue

Newspaper

Brown acrylic paint

White acrylic patching cement

Glossy interior varnish

Large-eye needle

String or ribbon

1. Cut two tusks from the upholstery foam, tapering them at the bottom for a more realistic tusk shape.

2. Crumple small pieces of aluminum foil into balls to form the walrus cheeks. Flatten out one side of the balls so that your real cheeks can fit underneath.

3. When your cheeks are formed, add one or two more layers of aluminum foil over them.

4. Decide how much space you'll need to have between your tusks so that they'll fall on either side of your mouth. Place the tusks on a flat surface with the correct amount of space in between. To form the base of the mask, cut strips of plaster gauze and place them over the front of the tusks. Wet your paintbrush and brush over the gauze. Add several layers of gauze, massaging each piece of gauze into the layer underneath it with the wet paintbrush. Allow the mask to dry.

5. After you've built up about five layers of gauze, position the aluminum foil cheeks evenly at the top of the tusks, overlapping the tusks a little.

6. Cut more gauze strips and dip them in water. Lay them across both cheeks and the top of the tusks to create a seam between the cheeks. Massage each strip into the layer beneath as you did before. You don't have to blend the cheeks into the tusks. It looks more natural to leave a defining edge between the cheeks, tusks, and chin.

7. Place several strips of the plaster gauze over the middle seam between the cheeks (this will be your nose).

8. When all of the plaster gauze is dry, trim any excess that is sticking out from behind the cheeks. Place one to three layers of plaster gauze over the edges that you have just trimmed.

9. Mix a solution of the white craft glue and water. Dip small strips of newspaper in the solution and layer the strips under the middle seam (nose) to create a chin.

10. When the mask has dried, paint the cheeks and the chin shades of brown using the acrylic paint.

11. Paint the tusks with several layers of acrylic patching cement making sure that you paint lengthwise. On the last layer of the patching cement, add a couple drops of the brown acrylic paint to each tusk. This will give the tusks an aged bone coloring.

12. When the paint and the patching cement are dry, paint the mask with a coat of the glossy interior varnish.

13. Poke a hole near the edge of each side of the mask with a large-eye needle. Thread string or a ribbon through the holes to secure the mask to your face.

A HALLOWEEN

Bestiary

MYTHICAL CREATURES & MONSTERS

There is a pantheon of mythical creatures from cultures around the world said to possess a range of powers from annoying or deceiving humans to obliterating them with the slightest glance.

Look to the creatures of folk legends and mythology for costume inspiration and ideas on how to bring out the beast in you.

ADARO
Spirits of the South Pacific, the Adaro were said to have the upper bodies of men and the tails of fish. They lived on the sun and traveled to the earth via rainbow. They could be mischievous (if there was rain on a sunny day, these creatures probably caused it) or malicious. They were said to attack humans with flying fish, knocking them unconscious or even killing them.

BAGINI
These creatures of Australian aboriginal mythology were beautiful half-human, half-animal spirit women with claw-like fingers and toes. They were said to capture and rape men, sometimes letting them go, but sometimes eating them.

CENTAUR
Considered savage and violent, the centaurs of Greek mythology were half-man and half-horse. They lived in the mountains and forests, attacked humans with rocks and branches, and feasted on raw flesh. Centaurs were also known for poor manners. They were drunken, lusty followers of Dionysus, the god of wine. Two centaurs, Chiron and Pholus, were kind and wise exceptions to the rule, and Chiron (the only immortal centaur) was even the tutor of many Greek heroes.

GOBLINS
The goblin originated in French legend and later showed up in cultures across Europe. Goblins dispositions ran the gamut from merely mischievous to downright diabolical. A smiling goblin could curdle blood, and its laughter could sour milk. In Scandinavia, the goblin Mara is said to have climbed into bed with men at night. In the morning, the men woke to find themselves completely unable to move or speak.

FURIES
Also known as the Erinyes or angry ones, these three hag-like female creatures from Greek mythology had dog heads, snake hair, and bat wings, and were often seen carrying whips. Their sole purpose was to chase after people and cause them horrible deaths.

HARPIES
In Greek mythology, these four female figures were wind spirits who carried the souls of the dead to Hades. Their names were Aello (Rain Squall), Celaeno (Storm Dark), Okypete (Swift Flying), and Podarge (Swift Foot). They had pale human faces, long hair, and brass claws. Everything they touched started to reek with an awful stench.

MEDUSA

Medusa was the only mortal of three beautiful sisters, the Gorgons. When she defiled the temple of Athena by having sex there with Poseidon, she was turned into a monstrous creature. Her hair was a nest of serpents and her body was covered in scales. She had bronze claw-like hands and golden wings. Anyone who saw her was immediately turned to stone. The hero Perseus eventually offed her by showing her her own reflection in a bronze shield, paralyzing her so that he could cut off her head.

MINOTAUR

Another creature from the Greeks, the minotaur had the body of a man and the head of a bull. The minotaur was supposedly the love child of the Queen of Crete and a bull with whom she fell in love after being enchanted by Poseidon. The Queen's husband, King Minos, built a labyrinth to hide the beast. The minotaur wandered around in the maze eating children until he was killed by the hero Theseus.

OGRES

Nearly every culture has some sort of ogre in their mythologies. The main tie between different ogres is that they all eat human flesh. Some Native American legends feature a cliff ogre, who would kick people over the edge of the cliff into the mouths of its hungry ogre-children who waited below. Negoogunogumbar was a Pygmy ogre who ate children, and the Japanese called their ogre Kijo.

SATYRS

Also known as Fauns, these half-goat (sometimes said to be half-deer), half-men were devotees of the forest god, Pan. Rather than evil, satyrs were mischievous and fun-loving (perhaps too much so, sometimes). Their man half was attractive, despite the horns and goat's beard. Satyrs liked to party and liked the ladies but didn't have such a bad reputation as the centaurs.

TROLLS

Scandinavian legends tell of gigantic man-eating creatures called trolls that live in the caves and forests of the mountains. Trolls are big; they have huge noses, ears, hands, and feet. The only thing small about a troll is its eyes. Experts say the best course of action during a troll encounter is to stop moving.
If you're lucky, the troll won't be able to find you.

UAM BAOZ

This half-man and half-octopus of Japanese folklore was the spirit of the oceans, capable of causing a tsunami.

Halloween Hard-wear

If you're more intimidated by a sewing machine than a high-speed power drill, don't despair—you can still make quite a costume on Halloween. You needn't enter a fabric store or even look at a needle and thread to assemble the outfits in this next section. They're mostly made from stuff you find around the house or at hardware or home improvement stores. While you're at your local mega-home center buying mulch, look around at all the fascinating, versatile materials that surround you. Duct tape, aluminum flashing, burlap, and lots of other supplies can be pressed into service with amazing results.

En Garde!
WEAPONS & ARMAMENTS

Besides making a costume scarier, weapons make a costume, well, more manly. It's a rare man who will venture into a craft store in search of costume materials. Men can find the materials for these weapons where they live—in the building materials department of a home improvement store. They're all made from aluminum flashing—the stuff used around gutters and on roofs. It's flexible, easy to cut, and looks a lot more like real metal than that fake plastic stuff used to make store-bought costume weapons.

You can make weapons to accessorize any kind of costume from any period of time. Just take a look at historical images in books or on-line to figure out the design for your armaments. When you've got a design in mind, just trace it onto a piece of flashing and cut it out with scissors. If the edges are too sharp and you're worried about actually harming someone, bind the sides with metal repair tape (which can also be found at home improvement or hardware stores and blends very well with flashing). To make your arms sturdier, it's best to cut out two identical pieces and hot glue them together.

Men of war need to protect themselves from blows to the head, so you'll need a helmet, too. The Viking-inspired helmet below is made from strips of aluminum flashing fitted to the wearer's head and held together with silver duct tape (or metal repair tape). Two bands cross on top of the head and attach to the central band that wraps around the head. To mimic the embellishments on a real Viking helmet, flat back marbles (all right, you probably do need to go to a craft store for those) were spray painted sliver and hot glued to the bands. Lush faux fur is duct taped in between the cross bands on the top to finish it off.

The mace that you see accompanying the helmet is made from a doggie chew toy spray painted silver, attached to a chain, and duct taped to a spray-painted dowel. *Very intimidating.*

The axe above is a great complement to a Viking costume. The axe shape is attached to a piece of black plastic piping with black electrical tape. The piping is lightweight, and like the other materials, it lives in home improvement stores.

An aluminum flashing scythe(in photo, page 72) is made by the same process and, of course, is the must-have accouterment for the grim reaper.

To give interest to this sword and make it sturdier, you can run a ballpoint pen down the center, causing it to fold and creating contours. Depending on the shape you choose, this sword could be used with a gladiator (page 20) or samurai costume (page 16), in which case you'd refer to it as a machete instead of a sword.

All armaments by Joan Morris

SIR BURLAP

Medieval reenactors spend small fortunes on replicas of chain mail and other knightly armaments. If you don't take your knighthood quite that seriously, you can create your own knightly attire with some stuff you have lying around the garage. This chain mail is made from burlap, spray-painted silver. The shin guards, arm cuffs, and helmet are made from aluminum flashing. The only other accessories you need are a few good stories about your imaginary knightly accomplishments. Make sure you throw in a few good ones about your pretend jousting titles and, if your audience is particularly hard to impress, your encounters with fellow knight Mick Jagger.

YOU WILL NEED

ROLL OF BURLAP

BALL POINT PEN

SCISSORS

FUSIBLE WEBBING AND IRON, SEWING MACHINE AND THREAD, OR SILVER ELECTRICAL TAPE

SILVER SPRAY PAINT

20-INCH (50.8CM) WIDE ALUMINUM FLASHING

HAMMER

LARGE NAIL

LEATHER CORD

SILVER TAPE

HOT GLUE GUN AND GLUE STICKS

Costume by Joan Morris

1. Lay the burlap on a flat surface and fold it in half.

2. Use one of your bigger shirts as a template to draw a tunic pattern on the burlap. Cut out the pattern, including a neck hole at the fold.

3. Bind the sides and the underside of the arms with fusible webbing and an iron (follow the manufacturer's instructions), a sewing machine and thread, or silver electrical tape.

4. Paint the burlap with the silver spray paint and let dry.

5. Look at pictures of medieval armor to figure out what your armor will look like. You'll need a breastplate and a back plate. When you have a design you like (the simpler the better), draw an outline of each shape on aluminum flashing and cut them out.

6. Working over a padded surface (such as a pillow), draw the contours of your breastplate design on the flashing with a pen. Press down hard so that the design will imprint correctly. The flashing will buckle outwards when you press on it with the pen. You'll wear the contoured side on the outside.

7. Make two holes on each shoulder and on the sides of the breast and back plates with a hammer and nail.

8. Use leather cord to tie the tunic and armor plates together through the holes you created in step 7.

9. On a piece of flashing, draw a rectangle shape with a flared top for the wrist cuff. Cut it out and repeat for the other arm.

10. Secure and close each cuff with silver tape and then hot glue one to each sleeve of the tunic.

11. Draw and cut oblong shin plates from the aluminum flashing.

12. Poke holes in the shin plates using the hammer and nail so that you can attach the plates over your shins with leather cord.

FOR THE HELMET

1. Cut six triangles from aluminum. Tape them together with silver duct tape, bending the flashing as necessary to create a round cap.

2. Fit a narrow piece of flashing to your head to serve as the band of the cap. When you've got the right size, cut it out and position it at the base of the cap. Fold a thin strip at the bottom underneath the cap and tape it in place.

3. Cut a long narrow strip that will extend down from the cap over your nose. Fold the top of the strip under the band of the cap and hot glue it in place.

YUKI ONA

Here's a wicked alternative to being a witch. Wear all white, and be the Yuki Ona. The Yuki Ona or Snow Woman is a she-demon of Japanese legend. She appears only during snowstorms, and some tales say she is the spirit of one who has died in the snow.

YOU WILL NEED

MEASURING TAPE

TILE FLOORING UNDERLAY

SCISSORS

HOT GLUE GUN AND GLUE STICKS

Costume by Joan Morris

The Yuki Ona is said to operate in one of several ways. Some stories say that she creates a snowstorm in order to leave travelers (always men) desperately lost. Beautiful, dressed in a white kimono, she then approaches the wayward man and asks him to hold her baby. Disoriented from the storm and bewitched by her beauty, the man fails to notice that she is floating in the air and has no feet. When he reaches out to her, he is frozen to death as her icy lips suck his life from him. In some stories, the Yuki Ona is said to approach men in isolated mountaintop cabins. She blows open the door of the cabin with her icy breath and either entices the men outside to steal their souls or freezes them in their beds.

This costume is made from flooring underlay which is composed of little white polystyrene balls that look like snow laminated in plastic. The material is stiff, so it will take any shape you cut it into. You can find it in home improvement stores, and it usually comes in big rolls. It will also come in handy when you redo the tile floor in your bathroom.

1. Measure from your shoulders to your feet to determine the length you need, then double it for a front and back piece, and add 2 feet (60.9 cm) for the kimono's train. Fold the underlay in half, leaving the extra length to one side for the back. Some flooring underlay comes with the manufacturer's label printed on it. You can cut it out, then hot glue another piece of the material behind it to fill the hole.

2. Cut out a circle big enough for your head and shoulders in the center of the fold.

3. Measure 12 inches (30.5 cm) in from each edge of the material and mark the spot. To make the sleeves, begin cutting 12 inches (30.5 cm) up from the bottom of the front of the kimono.

4. Use the hot glue gun to seal the sides and to create the sleeves.

5. Make spiky uneven cuts at the bottom of the dress, at the ends of the sleeves, and on the train.

6. Make a headpiece from a remaining scrap of the material. Hold a piece around your head and cut it to the appropriate measurement, then tape it together. Cut the top into points and contours on the bottom to fit the headpiece over your face. We added a snowflake Christmas ornament for more interest. Snowflakes also make great accessories for this costume.

LANDS-CAPES

Here's a perfect last-minute solution for the homeowner with an aversion to fabric stores. Go out to your garden shed and grab a roll of landscape fabric—you know, that black material that you put down in your flowerbeds to keep weeds away. Decide what kind of caped creature you are—a superhero? Witch or wizard? Bat? Make a landscape fabric cape and add your own black attire underneath. You'll have a costume in less than an hour, and next spring, you can recycle it right back into your garden.

YOU WILL NEED

MEASURING TAPE

LANDSCAPE FABRIC

SCISSORS

BLACK CORD

HOT GLUE GUN AND GLUE STICKS

STAPLER AND STAPLES

FELT SQUARES OR FABRIC REMNANTS

BLACK ELECTRICAL TAPE

POSTER BOARD (OPTIONAL)

BALLPOINT PEN (OPTIONAL)

SPRAY ADHESIVE (OPTIONAL)

All capes by Joan Morris

SUPERHERO CAPE

1. Measure and cut a piece of landscape fabric suitable for your height and width. Superhero capes tend to fall about mid-thigh. In terms of width, make sure it's wide enough to extend beyond your body with a little added fullness (you are going to have to fly in this thing, after all).

2. Fold the top edge of the landscape fabric over 3 inches (7.6 cm). Lay a piece of black cord inside the fold. Hot glue, staple, or tape down the flap to encase the cord.

3. Create your superhero emblem and hot glue it to the center back of the cape. If this is a really, really last minute costume, use an "S" and wear the cape over your regular work clothes. You'll be super-whatever-your-job-is: super accountant, super horticulturist, super administrative assistant—you get the picture.

BAT CAPE

1. Cut a piece of the black landscape fabric long enough to reach your knees and wide enough to wrap around you twice. Fold it in half.

2. Cut out half circles all the way around the bottom edge of the cape. This will give the bottom of the cape a scalloped edge.

3. Cut out a half circle in the middle of the fold for your neck.

4. Fold a 3-inch (7.6 cm) flap over at the neck and place a piece of black cord under the fold (leave a little bit sticking out on either end). Use black electrical tape to secure the flap and create a cord pocket.

OPTIONAL COLLAR *for* BAT *or* WITCH COSTUME

1. Draw the collar shape on the poster board and cut it.

2. Center the shape on a piece of landscape fabric. Cut out two pieces of landscape fabric 1 inch (2.5 cm) larger than the poster board piece.

3. Cut out an extra strip of landscape fabric for the collar's tie.

4. Using spray adhesive, attach one piece of landscape fabric to the collar shape and tuck the edges over onto the other side.

5. Attach the remaining piece of landscape fabric on the other side of the collar and trim it to fit. Attach the collar's tie.

WIZARD *or* WITCH

1. Cut two pieces of landscape fabric, long enough to reach your ankles and wide enough to wrap around your body twice with a little extra material for fullness. Glue the top edges of the two pieces together with hot glue (one side will be the lining of the cape).

2. Fold the top edge over 5 inches (12.7 cm) and place a piece of black cord under the fold with a little bit sticking out on each side. Hot glue the flap in place to create a cord pocket, or use black electrical tape instead.

MAGIC WAND

Create your own reality. With the stroke of your magic wand, you can transform yourself into a wizard, a good witch, a fairy, or if you had a bad week at work, an evil sorcerer or sorceress. With the power of the wand, you may even be able to change a stick-in-the-mud party partner into a charming companion for the evening.

Pretty much any stick-shaped object can be made into a wand. An easy solution is a wooden dowel from a hardware store. You can wrap fabric around the dowel or spray paint it silver or gold. For this sparkly number, Trulee Grace Hall wrapped a dowel with sparkly gold material, then wound a jewelry wire up the shaft, adding beads as she went. The top of the wire was bent into a star shape embellished with beads secured in place with a tiny dab of hot glue. Dangling ribbons can be wrapped under the wire to give the wand more swish.

Wand by Trulee Grace Hall

HAUNTINGLY FAMILIAR:
WITCHES & THEIR LITTLE HELPERS

During the Middle Ages when witch hysteria was at its height, common folks saw witches everywhere and witchcraft in everything. It wasn't enough that one's neighbor could be a witch. A stray cat or dog which appeared near the scene of mischief or mayhem could be a familiar, sent by a witch to do her evil bidding.

The word familiar comes from the Latin *famulus*, or attendant. Familiars were said to be minor demons or imps that took the shape of an animal and were given to witches by the devil or other witches to help them accomplish their wicked goals. Familiars were said to be kept alive by sucking blood from a witch's finger or wart. A familiar's job decription was wide-ranging: run errands, deliver messages, enchant, bewitch, or generally stir up trouble. For a witch, the advantages of using a familiar were obvious: a small animal could slip into and out of places where her presence would be too conspicuous. Witches could get a lot more done with the aid of these little assistants.

In Europe and North America, cats were the animals most identified as familiars. Perhaps because of their sneaking movements and aloof nature, people in the Middle Ages thought cats were in league with the devil. The glow in a cat's eye was said to prove its possession by demons. In the fifteenth century, Pope Innocent VIII declared that all cats were witches' familiars, and owning one was punishable by death. Millions of cats were killed all over Europe for this reason.

Cats were certainly not the only animals thought to be used by witches as familiars. Perhaps surprisingly, toads top the list of witches' familiars in medieval stories. Toads were strongly associated with the devil; in fact, it was said that when the devil chose to turn himself into an animal, the toad was his first choice. Toad parts were said to be common ingredients in witch potions: Basque witches reportedly used toad excrement in flying potions, toad spittle was part of a common invisibility spell, and "toad's milk," a real hallucinogenic substance secreted by toads in distress, was said to be used by witches to drug their victims. The witches in Macbeth included "toe of frog" in the concoction they brewed for the Danish prince. Witches were said to kiss the mouths of toads, baptize them, dress them in black velvet, festoon them with little bells, feed them elaborate meals, and teach them to dance. The toad's uncomely appearance may account for its association with evil. The horns seen in one species of toad were thought to be evidence of the animal's connection with the devil.

Beyond cats and toads, plenty of other animals were thought to be used as familiars: rabbits, dogs, wolves, weasels, ferrets, snakes, blackbirds, owls, spiders, flies, and chickens. The first witch in Macbeth had a cat named Graymalkin as a familiar, while the second had a "hedge-pig" named Paddock, and the third an owl named Harpier. In Japan, witches were said to pair up with foxes, while in Africa they were aided by hyenas or baboons.

Sometimes witch hunters took the familiar story one step further and accused witches of actually turning themselves into animals. In order to attend their midnight meetings with the devil undetected, witches were said to shape-shift into cats or rabbits.

Modern-day witches describe familiars as magical helpers with whom they have a psychic connection. Rather than going out and doing evil, familiars are said to warn a witch of danger, protect her, and defend her. The healing power of the animal is stressed rather than its power for destruction. This interpretation is more in line with Native American beliefs in totem animals, such as bears or wolves, which shaman or medicine men use as spirit guides in rites of passage or healing rituals.

Costume by Allison Smith

DOG IN DISGUISE

Few doting pet lovers could resist the urge to see their beloved companions dressed in a really cute costume like this one. Designer Allison Smith turned her dog Kobe into a sultan for Halloween by cutting up an old shirt to make a cape and turban. The rhinestones are hot glued to the fabric and outlined with glitter glue. As pampered as a pasha in his stunning ensemble, Kobe refuses to perform tricks in exchange for Halloween treats.

CAT ON THE RUN

While Kobe sat obediently for his close up, Elliot the cat had other ideas. A black cat jumping from a pumpkin shell is an adorable Halloween image, but despite bribes of yogurt and other inducements, Elliot was an unwilling model.

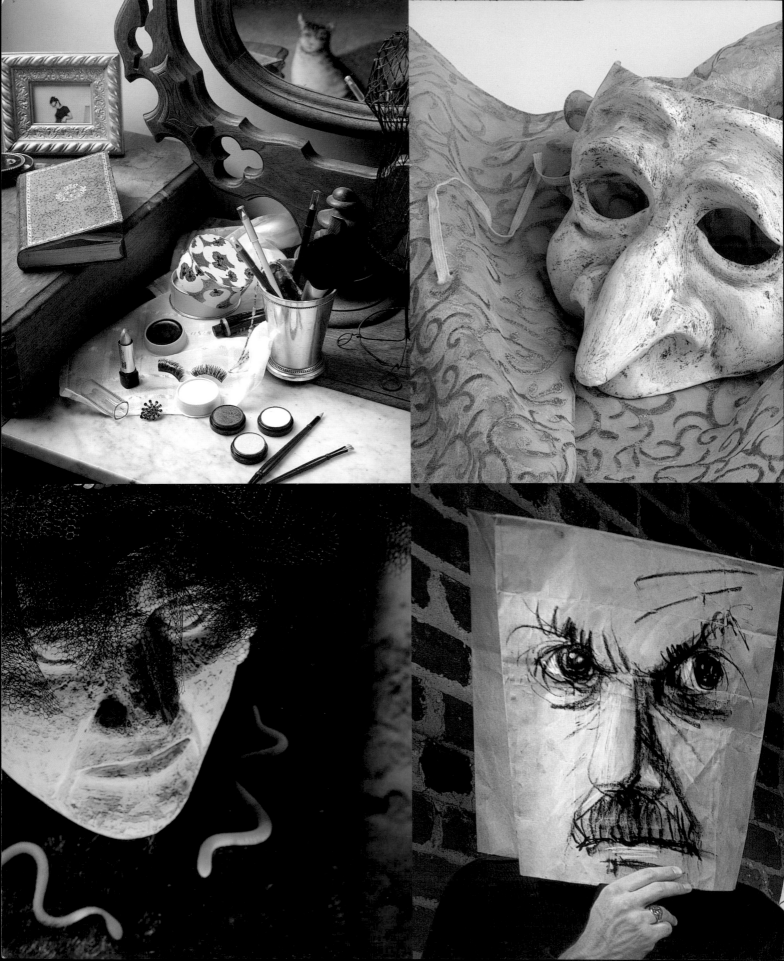

Hats, Masks, & Face Painting

Use your head on Halloween. Hats, masks, and face painting are great solutions to complement a costume or substitute for one if you can't quite pull a whole look together. From sassy to sinister, here's a collection of terrrific toppers, dazzling disguises, and lurid looks that's sure to turn heads.

MEDUSA WIG

Even on your worst hair day, you couldn't come close to Medusa's problems. Her hair was a nest of snakes that writhed and slithered around on her head, arching up and hissing as people approached. She looked so bad that people turned to stone when they saw her. Ordinarily, this is not a look that you would want to emulate, but on Halloween, the ghastlier the better. A black sheet, curtain, or cape worn with your snake wig would make a complete costume.

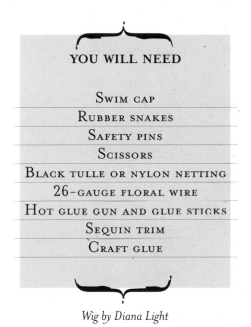

YOU WILL NEED

SWIM CAP

RUBBER SNAKES

SAFETY PINS

SCISSORS

BLACK TULLE OR NYLON NETTING

26-GAUGE FLORAL WIRE

HOT GLUE GUN AND GLUE STICKS

SEQUIN TRIM

CRAFT GLUE

Wig by Diana Light

1. Use as many rubber snakes as you can find. If you don't like their color, spray paint them black. Position them around the swim cap with their heads pointing out in all directions. Pin them to the cap with safety pins.

2. Cut the tulle or nylon netting into little strips. Fold the strip and scrunch the middle together. While holding the piece in a scrunched-up ball in one hand, pin it to the cap with your other hand. When you release your hand, the tulle will stretch out, creating a full "nest" look for the snakes to sit on. Keep adding these balls of tulle until the whole cap is covered.

3. Attach black sequin trim to the netting in intervals around the cap (it will look like more snakes coming out of the nest).

4. Cut the floral wire into several pieces and hot glue a piece of sequin trim to each side of each piece of wire. Bend the wires into snake shapes and hot glue one end of each wire to the cap.

VIDEO TAPE WITCH WIG

Face it—you are never going to actually watch that trendy exercise video tape again. You can continue to let it sit there and make you feel guilty, or you can get some use out of it and make it into a witch wig. You'll have fun breaking it open and pulling out the tape, knowing that you will never again have to watch those hard-bodied exercise nuts outpace you again.

YOU WILL NEED

OLD VIDEO
SCREWDRIVER
SCISSORS
PLASTIC MESH ONION SACK,
SOFT OR STIFF
WITCH'S HAT

Wig by Lois Simbach

1. Dismantle the plastic case of the video with a screwdriver. Don't try to break the plastic casing off the video-tape, as it will leave sharp edges that could be dangerous.

2. Take the tape off the roll and measure off whatever lengths you want, double them, and then cut them. Knot the tape securely to the mesh using double knots (loose knots won't hold the slick surface of the tape).

3. Continue knotting tape to the sack, making the wig as thick as you like. You don't have to cover the top portion of the sack because you will have a hat on.

4. Pull the sack over your head and add the witch's hat. Your witch wig is clearly superior to the store-bought kind.

Love the hair!

CONE HEADS

A cone-shaped hat is simplicity itself. It's also a versatile topper for a number of Halloween costumes: witch, wizard, medieval princess, garden gnome, or, if you have great self-esteem and aren't worried about being taunted, a dunce cap.

LEFT

WIZARD'S HAT

The base of the hat is just a piece of poster board, like the kind used for kids' school projects. You can find it in discount stores and even in the school supplies aisle of the grocery store.

To fit the hat, just hold the poster board up to your head to gauge the size you'll need and mark the spot where the sides meet. Use the marks as a guide to draw the base of a triangle, then mark the sides of the triangle up in a point as high as you like, and cut out the triangle. Use a beautiful piece of royal blue or purple velveteen for this hat (you'll use less than 1 yard [91.4 cm]). Lay the triangle in the center of the fabric, then cut it, leaving a 1-inch (2.5 cm) border all around.

Spray the back of the fabric with spray adhesive, then carefully center it over the triangle, smoothing out any wrinkles as you press it down. Press the borders over the backside of the triangle. Form the cone and hold the two sides together with strong paper clips (you'll probably need to place something inside the cone as a weight to keep it in place). Run a line of hot glue along the edge of one side and press the other side down to secure it. Once the glue has dried, remove the clips.

Add the magic looking glass (otherwise known as flat-backed marbles) to the hat in a random pattern with hot glue. Add a silver Christmas ornament stuck through the opening at the top of the cone and secure it with hot glue.

To complete your wizard costume, wrap yourself in a dark blue or purple sheet and hot glue a little white faux fur around the border.

CENTER

GNOME

While perusing the flooring tile department of your local mega home-improvement store, you may come upon this fantastic cone-shaped item: a grout bag. It's inexpensive, spray-paintable, and cries out to become the pointy hat of a garden gnome. After you've located one, walk over to the paint aisle and get a can of spray paint in garden gnome red. You should be able to cover the cap with one coat. To complete your garden gnome ensemble, add a loose-fitting blue sweatshirt, brown pants and boots, a belt, and a beard. Once Halloween is over, you can store the bag in your garage and use it next time you need to regrout your bathroom.

RIGHT

MEDIEVAL PRINCESS HAT

This hat is made in the same way as the wizard's hat. You could add a sheer scarf poking out from the top of the point, or add a brim and make it into a witch's hat. This pretty but slightly mysterious fabric could go either way.

TUTTI-*Fruitti* HAT

Skeletons, vampires, and other undead creatures can get to be such a downer after a while—all that black and ashen skin is anything but uplifting. You can truly be the "life" of the party if your costume includes a tropical hat like this one. This is a no-sew hat that you can make in just a few minutes. Add a peasant blouse, a full red skirt, some hoop earrings, and a pair of maracas to complete your sultry showgirl look.

Hat by Diana Light

1. Hot glue the paper plates together back-to-back.

2. Fold the red material in half lengthwise to find the middle and mark it. Make a diagonal line from the center to the edges until you have a traced a large triangle on the material then cut out the triangle.

3. Tuck a hem under on all sides and secure it in place with hot glue.

4. Put the fused plate under the triangle, centered on the longest side, about 3 1/4 inches (8.2 cm) from the edge. Lay a line of hot glue on the fused plate and then press the triangle in place.

5. Hot glue the yellow rickrack a little in from the edge of the longest side of the triangle.

6. Arrange the plastic fruit in a pyramid so that you can pile as much of it on the hat as possible. Attach the bottom layer of the pyramid to the fabric with hot glue.

7. Continue stacking the fruit in a pyramid, gluing it on with the cyanoacrylate glue. Do not try to use the hot glue gun, as the glue will peel off between the two plastics. Fill in the holes between the fruits with small groups of plastic grapes or berries. Remember to look at the fruit from all directions to keep it balanced. It will also be much easier to wear.

8. To wear the hat, place one of the plates on your head, wrap the ends of the triangle around the back of your head, and tie it, or bring the ends back to the front and tie it there. Tuck the excess fabric hanging in the back up over the crossed ends.

HEADLINERS

Use your head as the focal point for your costume. These easy-to-make toppers start with a simple circle, embellished to suit your needs.

Wreath by Diana Light

A Greek or Roman costume, for mortals or gods, can consist of little more than an expertly wrapped bed sheet with a gold rope sash and a wreath like this one. Use floral wire as a base, twisting as many pieces as you need end-to-end to fit around your head. Once you've got a continuous circle, wrap the wire in floral tape to strengthen it. Add silk leaves (you can either find gold ones or spray paint ordinary ones gold) by wrapping a gold ribbon around the piece and tucking the leaves under and wrapping again at regular intervals around the headpiece.

A heavenly halo fit for an angel or saint is also easy to make—no sewing required. Create the halo base the same way you do for the Roman wreath, by joining pieces of floral wire together end on end to make a circle that fits your head. Wrap floral tape around the circle as you do with the wreath. Make another larger circle that will serve as the halo, and tape it (standing up) to the back of your headpiece with floral tape. Cut a circle of sparkly gold fabric to cover the circle, leaving an extra border around the edges that you can tuck over the back and hot glue down. Hot glue a piece of gold trim around the halo for a finishing touch. Wrap the head-piece circle with pipe cleaners, and then hot glue gold trim on top of it. An artfully folded white sheet can serve as your angel garb, and the wings on page 23 can be cut in an angelic shape to complete your costume.

Halo by Diana Light

If you have royal aspirations, make a crown. The base for this one is a piece of cardboard cut to fit your head. Cover it with shiny gold fabric, leaving enough room to attach the two ends together to form a ring. Hot glue beads around the outside of the crown, then wrap a thin jewelry wire around the crown, shaping flourishes with needle-nose pliers and threading beads up and around the wire. Experiment with twists, bends, and curls.

Crown by Trulee Grace Hall

For a woodland nymph, fairy, or other spirit of the forest, a length of grapevine (available at craft stores) embellished with a delicate silk leaf garland is the perfect topper. Hot glue acorns (real or decorative) around the garland for extra dimension. Add other wood-land embellishments to a fairy dress like the one on page 26, and you'll be positively enchanting.

Wreath by Diana Light

RIBBON WIG HAT

You've got your Marie Antoinette costume ready to go, but don't have
time or skill to tease your hair into a fabulous baroque
pile of ringlets. Don't panic—you can fake it with a ribbon wig hat.
This clever design is the brainchild of New Orleans milliner
Tracy Thomson, who makes them for Mardi Gras and Halloween.
It's a deceptively simple idea. Get a few spools of gift ribbon
in the width and texture of your choice. White is great for a
powdered wig look, but black ribbon makes for a spectacular
witch or she-vampire wig.

Wig hat by Tracy Thompson

While you're sitting on the couch watching TV, start curling the ribbon by holding it tight on one end and running a closed pair of scissors down one side. When you've got a good pile, start gluing the ribbon to a hat form. A relatively stiff, rounded form with no brim works best. You can work over a thrift store find; just make sure that the hat won't look conspicuous under your wig (you may need to spray paint it to match). Experiment with different glues to find out which one holds your ribbon the best. Hot glue will probably melt your ribbon, so don't try it. Strong tacky glue is a better choice. Continue gluing ribbon around the hat until you're happy with the results. You can keep filling in ribbons to make the wig fuller. When you're done, add some feathers or ribbons in your "hair" for more drama.

BASIC PLASTER FACE MASK

To make a plaster mask, you first need to find a partner to assist you. This is a great project for a couple to do together so you can trade off being the model and the maker. This is a very easy process to complete if you have the right materials.

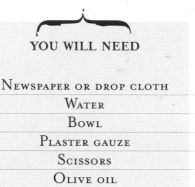

YOU WILL NEED

NEWSPAPER OR DROP CLOTH
WATER
BOWL
PLASTER GAUZE
SCISSORS
OLIVE OIL

*Available at craft or medical supply stores. If you cannot find it, you can substitute strips of cotton gauze dipped in plaster of Paris.

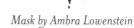

Mask by Ambra Lowenstein

1. Set up a workspace covered with drop cloths. The model will need to be in position and comfortable for about 20 minutes. Keep the plaster and water close at hand near the model and over the drop cloth.

2. Cut the gauze into strips of a variety of different shapes and sizes, for example, 1 x 3-inch (2.5 x 7.6 cm) rectangles or 1-inch (2.5 cm) squares.

3. Coat the mask model's face with olive oil or another vegetable oil. Apply a generous amount of oil to the eyebrows, lashes, and hairline to prevent the plaster from sticking to the hair. Don't rub the oil deeply into the skin. It's meant only to be a protective layer.

4. Dip a large strip of plaster in the water (shaking off any excess) and lay it on the model's oiled face. Rub the strip lightly to smooth it. Continue this process using the different sizes of plaster for the appropriate areas of face. Make sure that each strip overlaps another and is bonded to all the strips it touches. Repeat the process until at least 3 layers of plaster have been applied to the entire face. Note: Leave openings over the eyes, nostrils, and mouth.

5. The model will need to remain still until the mask dries. The model should then contort his or her facial muscles until the mask pops off. Sometimes, even when lots of oil has been used, an area of the mask will still stay stuck to the face. The model should continue to make expressive faces, the funnier the better, until the mask can be gently pulled off. Remember that the mask is still very delicate. After the mask has been removed, set it nose-side down, and allow the model to clean up.

KABUKI 07
CHINESE THEATRE MASK

Follow the instructions for making a basic plaster mask, but add aluminum foil to accentuate the nose and chin. Just crumple the foil into balls and place the balls on the finished mask. Cover them with strips of plaster to seal them into the mask. Continue adding plaster strips until all the features have been enhanced and no foil is left showing. Let the mask dry for 24 hours.

Build up the surface of the mask with papier mâché by dipping strips of newspaper in a water and glue mixture and laying them on top of the mask. Continue until you've covered the surface of the mask,

making sure you reinforce the eye, nose, and mouth areas, and that the paper lies flush to mask and creates a smooth surface with no stray pieces sticking up. After the mask has dried, brush on an extra layer of glue and water solution to create a smooth surface.

Paint the mask with several layers of white acrylic paint. Use a pencil to draw the lines for the face pattern, and fill in the lines with black and red acrylic paint and an ultra fine paintbrush. Coat the mask with a layer of varnish when you're done to protect it, then drill two small holes near the outer edges and string a ribbon or piece of elastic through the holes to attach it to your head.

Mask by Ambra Lowenstein

COPYRIGHT-FREE IMAGE MASKS

Here's a way to use some of the wonderful pre-existing imagery out there on-line or in books without having to worry about a lawsuit.

Find a copyright-free image. Graphics that are more than 70 years old usually are, but double-check to make sure. Clip art images or engravings taken from books or web sites are good sources. Enlarge the image (you may need to go to a copy shop to get the image as large as you need it for a mask). Mount the image on foam-core board with adhesive spray, then carefully cut around it with a craft knife. Color and embellish it as you wish. Use a flat paint stirring stick as a holder. Decorate your mask as desired (felt-tipped markers work well), then simply glue it to the stick. If you like, you can cut out eye holes. Not only is this an easy on and off mask, it can also be used a fan in a hot, crowded roomful of revelers.

Masks by Terry Taylor

SIMPLE MASK

A basic premade black or white half-mask (available at craft stores) can be the base for any fantasy mask you can imagine. For a clean and elegant look, embellish a white mask with flowers—simply hot glue silk or other artificial flowers to the edges or the entire surface. Designer Terry Taylor added white sequin tape at the base of the flower petals on this mask for a more polished look. For more mystery, he hot glued a veil to the bottom back edge of the mask. A premade mask base is also a perfect foundation for a leaf mask (see page 37) in the colors of summer or autumn. Leaves spray-painted gold or silver also make a dramatic impression. If you're going for a more sinister look, try a black premade mask base and add black or dark feathers.

My! What a beak!

BIRD MASK

Alfred Hitchcock's 1960s film did
a lot to change the popular perception
of birds. While we're used to thinking
of our feathered friends as cheerful
creatures, there's always the shadow
of a doubt. Under the right circumstances, could that harmless-looking
chick-a-dee out your window become
a ruthless killer? Its beak a lethal
weapon? This slightly sinister
bird beak mask, worn with an all
black ensemble and some black
feathered wings, will set spines to
shuddering all around you.

YOU WILL NEED

SUPPLIES FOR PLASTER MASK
(SEE PAGE 96)

MEDIUM-WEIGHT CARDBOARD

SCISSORS

PENCIL

HOT GLUE GUN AND GLUE STICKS

NEWSPAPER

CRAFT GLUE

PAINTBRUSHES

ACRYLIC PAINT

HAIRSPRAY

FEATHERS

ELASTIC CORD

POWER DRILL (OPTIONAL)

Mask by Ambra Lowenstein

1. Follow the instructions for the plaster face mask on page 96.

2. Cut two elongated triangles (as long as you like) from cardboard to serve as your beak. Keep in mind that if your beak is too long, you'll have to stand quite far from people when you talk to them.

3. Fold each triangle down the center. Holding the triangles up to the mask, measure the angle at which the triangles fit closest to the mask and mark line with a pencil. Cut the cardboard along lines so that two triangles fit together and lay flat against the mask. Hot glue the triangles in place on the mask.

4. Cover the entire beak with plaster strips, reinforcing the seam between the face mask and the beak. Use some extra plaster strips to build up a smooth, raised ridge around the eye holes. Let dry for 24 hours.

5. Tear newspaper into small pieces (½ x 1 inch, [1.3 x 2.5 cm], square and strips). Build up the surface of the mask by placing each strip on the mask and painting over it with a glue and water solution. The paper should be flush to the mask to create a smooth surface. Cover one section of the mask at a time, making sure to add extra layers around the eyes, seams and outer rim for added support. When you've covered the whole mask, paint a layer of the glue and water solution over entire surface. Let dry completely.

6. Quickly brush on an extra layer of glue and water solution and allow to dry again.

7. Paint the mask in the design of your choice.

8. Hot glue feathers to the face of the mask. Begin with the center feathers (closest to beak) and work your way out to exterior edge of mask using your nicest shaped feathers in the most prominent areas.

9. Spray the feathered section with a thin coat of aerosol hairspray. Paint a layer of varnish over beak.

10. Hot glue a piece of elastic cord or ribbon to the back of the mask to secure it to your head. You could also drill a hole at each edge of the mask and thread the cord or ribbon through the holes.

PAPER BAG MASKS

In the 1960s, New York artist Saul Steinberg created a series of brown paper bags masks and had his friends photographed wearing them in party scenes or just going about their daily lives. Steinberg's theory behind the project was that everyone wears a mask, whether real or metaphorical. Atlanta artist Joe Peregine and his students created these masks. Each artist drew an interpretation of a friend while observing his or her face as the model watched TV. These simple masks express so much emotion, and are especially effective when worn with no costume at all. If you host a Halloween party, try providing guests with a paper bag and drawing supplies so that they can draw each other as a mask. They may not be able to wear the mask all night, but it will certainly make for a great photo opportunity.

CLASSIC MASKS
of
COMMEDIA DELL'ARTE

From animated cartoon characters to big-screen buffoons, most modern comic figures can trace their roots to the masked characters of *commedia dell'arte*, the original form of improvisational comedy. Starting in Italy in the 16th century, troupes of commedia dell'arte actors traveled around Europe playing instantly recognized stock characters in improvised scenes. Across cultures and languages, audiences knew the characters by their masks, which were central to the character's personality. Although each troupe developed variations on the masks, the basic characteristics remained the same and expressed the character's personality. Even today, a pompous academic is often depicted with a large nose, and a scheming character with small eyes and furrowed brows.

EL CAPITANO
Braggart character with huge, putty-like nose mask. Usually wears a uniform, but avoids battle. Struts and swaggers while boasting of his imaginary accomplishments.

PULCHINELLA (PUNCH)
A rascal who was always creating trouble, this character later developed into the Punch puppet, familiar to people from Punch and Judy shows. Pulchinella wore white trousers, a large white shirt and a conical hat. His black half-mask featured a melancholy expression.

PANTALONE
Greedy merchant character usually dressed in tight clothes in a vain attempt to attract women. His mask features a long, pointed nose that curves downward.

IL DOTTORE
Pompous academic character usually seen wearing a black academic gown. His mask covers only the forehead and nose. The nose of the mask was bulbous to imply heavy drinking.

ARLECCHINO (HARLEQUIN)
Servant character who wears a costume in a diamond pattern that became synonymous with his name. This character's black mask looks a like a cat's face—small eyes, low forehead, and furrowed brows, expressing cunning intent.

WITCH, VAMPIRE, *or* FRANKENSTEIN'S BRIDE

YOU WILL NEED

MAKEUP SPONGE

PANCAKE MAKEUP OR OTHER BASE

GREEN POWDER EYE SHADOW
(OPTIONAL)

GREEN, BLACK, DARK GREEN, OR
DARK BROWN LIQUID EYE SHADOW

MAKEUP BRUSHES

DARK GRAY OR CHARCOAL POWDER
EYE SHADOW

Photo illustration by Brigid Burns

1. Using a sponge, apply a thick layer of very white pancake make-up to your whole face. If you're going for a green-skin look, use liquid base colored with a touch of green powder. You can also find specialty concealer products that come in a very pale shade of green.

2. Create a thick, elongated eye-brow shape over your own eye-brow with dark liquid eye shadow. Curve the ends of the brow out and up. Shade under the brow, under your lower lashes, alongside your nose, and under your cheek-bones with charcoal gray shadow.

3. Using the same liquid shadow you used to create the brow, create lines radiating out from the brow. You can also make the lines look like very thick or shaggy brow hair. Underline your eyes in the same color, and create lines extending down from the liner across your cheeks.

4. Create a false lip outline that looks like two mountain peaks over your lips. Use the same color you used for your brows.

SKULL, SKELETON, or GRIM REAPER

YOU WILL NEED

MAKEUP SPONGE

MAKEUP BRUSHES

WHITE PANCAKE MAKEUP OR OTHER
BASE

GREEN POWDER EYE SHADOW
(OPTIONAL)

BLACK LIQUID EYELINER

BLACK LIPSTICK

LOOSE POWDER

WHITE LIQUID EYE SHADOW BASE*

WHITE CONCEALER STICK
(OPTIONAL)

* A product designed to go under
eye shadow so that it stays on longer

1. Sponge on a
thick coat of very
white pancake makeup.
You can add a little
green around the edges
if you like by adding
green powdered eye
shadow to a liquid base and
sponging the mixture on
around the edge of your
face.

2. Paint large black circles
around your eyes with black liquid eyeliner (it comes with it's
own brush). Create the outline
first, then fill it in, closing your
eyes as you paint over your eyelids.

3. Paint two triangles on either side of
your nose with the black eyeliner.

4. Outline a large oblong shape around
your mouth with black eyeliner. Fill in the
shape with black lipstick. Brush a layer of
powder over the layer. Create a series of white
"teeth" over the shape using a makeup brush
and the white liquid eye shadow base. You can
also use a white
concealer stick for this process.

5. Use your black liquid eyeliner to create
cracks across your forehead and cheeks if
desired.

KABUKI ACTOR

or

CHINESE OPERA STAR

YOU WILL NEED

Makeup sponge
Makeup brushes
Pancake makeup or other base
Red lipstick
Loose powder
Black liquid eyeliner

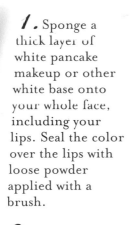

1. Sponge a thick layer of white pancake makeup or other white base onto your whole face, including your lips. Seal the color over the lips with loose powder applied with a brush.

2. Use a makeup brush to apply a thick line of red lipstick from the area where your eyebrow starts, moving down to the center of your nose, then back up, under your eye, and out to the edge of your face.

3. Paint your upper lip with the red lipstick, but leave the bottom one white. Add two teardrop shapes at the edge your mouth so they look as though they are an extension of the red upper lip.

4. Use the black liquid eyeliner to make thick brows over your own brows and extending upward, tapering at the end.

Decor

As September comes to an end, smiling scarecrows start to crop up on suburban lawns and jack-o'lanterns appear in the windows of city apartments. Spider webs and bats hang from doors in schools and offices. 'Tis the season of Halloween.

Decorating homes and yards for Halloween has become almost as common as putting up Christmas trees. In the past, Halloween was celebrated on just one night. Now Halloween lovers start preparing for the magical night weeks in advance. The stores are bursting with Halloween decorations from August on, but if you're looking for something beyond the standard pre-fab options, keep reading.

We've assembled a collection of decorating ideas and projects that are spooky, sophisticated, and definitely different. If your pumpkin decorating methods have become a little stale, we've got some fresh ideas that will rekindle your enthusiasm for this time-honored tradition. You're not limited to pumpkins, either. You can make funny or frightening faces on plenty of vegetables. Creating corn dollies is a tradition older than Halloween itself. We'll show you how to make one that's dramatically different. A giant spider that can weather the elements and eyes that light the way for your trick-or-treaters will make an unforgettable impact on Halloween night. Whether your taste tends toward the frightful or delightful, you'll find ideas that you can really use.

Pumpkin Carving Basics

Immortal Italian sculptor Michelangelo said that in every chunk of marble a beautiful figure waited to be freed by the sculptor's hand. The same can be said about pumpkins. It's up to you to channel the master and unleash your pumpkin's latent personality.

Free-spirited Halloween enthusiasts may drill, paint, stencil, skewer, or stamp, a pumpkin, but if you're a pumpkin purist, you've got to carve. Here are a few suggestions for making the best of this time-honored, much-anticipated yearly, tradition.

TOOLS

If you the pick the right tools, you'll have a much easier time carving your pumpkin. Some experts advise using a special pumpkin-carving tool set, but it's really not necessary. You should be able to carve any pumpkin with supplies you already have at home. Here's a list of some pumpkin carving tools and what they're used for:

GENERAL CARVING

Long, thin-bladed knife
Boning knife

CARVING SMALL OR FINE DETAILS

Paring knife
Mini-saw
Craft knife
Linoleum carving or woodcarving tools

CARVING THE SURFACE OF THE SKIN

Wood gouge
Wood chisel
Melon baller

CREATING ROUND HOLES

Electric drill
Awl, ice pick, or nail

Sharp-ended pipes
Clay-cutting tools

SCOOPING OUT THE CENTER

Spoon
Ladle
Ice cream scoop

1. Decide which surface of the pumpkin to carve. Generally, you'll want the smoothest, roundest side. If your pumpkin has mottling or defects on all sides, work them into your design or carve them out.

2. Create an opening so that you can remove the insides and insert your light source. If you plan to light your jack-o' lantern with a candle, you'll want to remove the top of the pumpkin so that you can insert it. Carve a hexagonal shape around the stem to remove the top. A hexagon gives the shape some angled sides so that it doesn't fall back into the. As you cut out the lid, angle the knife so that hole will be somewhat cone shaped. If you're going to light your pumpkin with minilights or a light-bulb, you'll want to insert them through the bottom or back of the pumpkin.

3. Once you've got an opening, hollow out the pumpkin. Usually, you can just use a spoon, but if the pumpkin flesh is very firm, you may want to use an ice cream scoop. Make sure that the walls of the pumpkin remain about 1 inch (2.5 cm) thick. Use the spoon to scrap the inside walls clean and discourage

bugs from gathering in your pumpkin. If you'll be using a candle, make sure that you have scrapped the bottom of the pumpkin flat, so that it won't tip over.

4. When you're ready to carve your design, you have several options for getting the image onto your pumpkin. If you're feeling confident, just carve freehand. If you need some extra guidance, draw the image you want to cut on the pumpkin with a marker. For a very complicated image, draw the design on paper, transfer it to the pumpkin by pin pricking the lines of the drawing to leave an outline on the pumpkin skin, then carve into the outline. Always begin carving from the center of the design outwards, since a pumpkin will become weaker each time you remove a piece. Push carved pieces out from the center of the pumpkin to remove them. If an extra piece breaks off accidentally, stick a toothpick in the back of the piece and push it back into place.

If you just want to make a design on the surface of the pumpkin without breaking the skin, use linoleum carving tool, wood gouge, or melon baller to etch your design into the surface.

5. Add your light source. If you want to use a candle, use a white one in a clear glass holder for maximum illumination. Insert your candle and place the lid back on the pumpkin. After a minute or so, remove the lid. You'll see a soot mark where the smoke from the candle tried to escape. Carve a hole in this position so that the smoke and heat from the candle will have an exit point. If an open flame makes you nervous, substitute minilights or light bulbs, glo-sticks, or battery-operated tap lights.

PUMPKIN LIFE PRESERVERS

*A*s fruits go, pumpkins are pretty hardy. Can you imagine subjecting an apple or a pear to the same treatment pumpkins receive? They'd be shriveled up in no time. Despite their robust nature, pumpkins sometimes need some TLC to save their skins (and their insides) after they've gone under the knife. Carving sucks moisture out of a pumpkin, and dehydrated pumpkins pucker and develop mold. The first, most obvious solution to keeping your pumpkin fresh is to wait until a day or two before Halloween to carve it. If Halloween spirit hits you early in the month and you just can't wait to carve, review the following ideas. With a few precautionary measures, your pumpkin will go the distance at Halloween, at least until the trouble-making teens down the street throw it into the street.

• Pick a pumpkin that's already completely ripe—those that are still a bit green will decompose more quickly after being carved.

• Carve the inside down to the sturdiest part of the rind. Leaving a lot of soft flesh inside attracts more bugs.

• After you carve your pumpkin, don some work gloves, grab some paper towels, and coat all the cut surfaces and the whole interior of the pumpkin with petroleum jelly. Petroleum jelly provides a protective barrier to seal in moisture. It's like giving your pumpkin a moisturizing facial.

• Let your carved pumpkin sit in a bucket of water overnight. Add a little bleach to the water to discourage the build-up of bacteria that leads to fungus and rot.

• If you have enough space, store your pumpkin in the refrigerator overnight to slow down decomposition.

• If you live in a hot climate, keep your pumpkin in a shady area during the day. Direct heat will contribute to dehydration.

• Purchase a pumpkin preservative product made especially to deter mold, rot, and bugs. You can find this product on-line or at larger nurseries where pumpkins are sold.

PUMPKIN PERSONALITIES

Beneath its thick orange skin, every pumpkin has a personality just waiting to be discovered. Is yours the happy-go-lucky type with big eyes and a wide smile or a sinister character with jagged teeth and a threatening look? Maybe your pumpkin doesn't even want a face, but prefers to remain abstract. The pumpkins in our collection represent a range of styles, from the traditional (with a twist) to the updated, the unadorned to the fanciful. Take a look at our pumpkins, then take a fresh look at yours and unlock its hidden potential.

NOSY PUMPKINS

This center pumpkin with the impish expression looks as though he's holding court, flanked by two serious-faced bodyguards. Use prominent stems as pumpkin proboscises when possible (try saying that three times fast). The red pepper nose on the pumpkin king was inserted through a perfectly round hole created by an apple corer. The more dramatic a pumpkin's nose, the less elaborate the rest of the facial features need to be. Simple slits or round circles won't distract, so an observant eye will focus on the nose. Since the stems are used as noses, there's not a traditional top to open. Cut a hole in the back of each pumpkin instead, and light them with minilights rather than candles.

PUMPKIN KING

The jolly old pumpkin king wears a crown of bittersweet vines and sits on a viney throne. Bittersweet accents add dimension and interest to your pumpkins.

GEOMETRIC PUMPKIN

If you're looking for something a little less representational in your pumpkin, try a geometric cutout pattern. These simple squares cast fascinating shadows on your walls.

BUSHY-HEADED PUMPKINS

Who says pumpkins have to be bald? Give your pumpkins a full head of hair by removing the top and inserting a bunch of fall grasses inside. Colorful fountain grass or pampas plumes are great for dimension and color. Use generous amounts of whatever grass you choose, lest your pumpkin appear to be wearing a comb-over. The bottoms of the stalks show through the carved mouths and look like teeth. Cut holes in the back of each pumpkin and illuminate them with minilights instead of candles for safety. This idea works best with long, tall pumpkins (rather than short, squatty ones).

PLATED PUMPKIN

White pumpkin varieties are somewhat rare and have poetic names like Lumina or Baby Boo. If you're lucky enough to find one of these exotic gems, you may not be able to bring yourself to cut into its beautiful surface. A white pumpkin, surrounded by mini-pumpkins on a plate, can make a delightful display without any further embellishment.

OUT OF THE PUMPKIN PATCH, INTO THE FLOWER BED

As late October approaches, a few hardy plants may hold on, but brown may be replacing green as the predominant color in your garden. Rather than restricting pumpkins to your porch and windowsill, why not place them around your garden for color? Uncarved, pumpkins can last for months, helping you ease the transition from fall into the barren winter. The coy cat cutout that creeps in front of this pumpkin was made with a scrap of wood and placed in the garden on seasonal patrol.

OFF THE TURNIP TRUCK

Turnips were the first jack-o'lanterns. If you want to get back to the roots of Halloween, try carving turnips or beets instead of pumpkins. After your first few attempts, you may discover why the Irish and Scots abandoned turnip carving in favor of the easier-to-carve pumpkin. But keep with it: a hollowed out and carved turnip or beet has a wonderful nostalgic quality. Use a paring knife, apple corer, and craft knife to successfully work on such a small scale. Since these root vegetables are markedly smaller than most pumpkins and don't have flat bottoms enabling easy display, think of creative ways to show them off. The points of a pitchfork are perfect for mounting these carved creations, plus pitchforks are another traditional symbol of Halloween.

TRI-POD PUMPKINS

A lot of thought goes into creating pumpkin faces, but what about the rest of their bodies? These squatty fellows look like pumpkins outfitted with three little legs, but they're actually a type of squash called Turk's turban. Try coaxing a smile from their wide, flat faces as an interesting alternative to a pumpkin. Turk's turbans have notoriously tough skin, so use a craft knife for more control when you carve them. Place a candle in front of, rather than inside, these squash to illuminate them. A grouping of several squash together makes a charming display.

THE UN-PUMPKINS

For a few weeks every fall, pumpkins become the undisputed stars of the produce department. As an amusing departure from tradition, shine the Halloween spotlight on some overlooked and underappreciated fruits and vegetables. Trulee Grace Hall created this appealing collection of un-pumpkins from apples, peppers, onions, gourds, squash, and various nuts and beans.

Unlock the inner personality of your fruits and vegetables with a few embellishments made from other kinds of produce. Cheerful, charming, roguish, goofy, strange, or mean—you'd be surprised at the emotional range that a vegetable can express.

Look for fruits or vegetables with interesting features or mutations. The sweet little apple creature is made from a single apple that looks like two fused together. A strange outgrowth on an eggplant makes a perfect nose. Gourds with lots of bumps and warts have an otherworldly quality that you can use to your advantage. Red pepper devil's ears accent a green pepper's contorted face, creating a very sinister look. For eyes and teeth, use black-eyed peas or other beans.

Un-pumpkins by Trulee Grace Hall

PUMPKINLESS JACK-O'LANTERNS

This lightweight lantern has all the advantages of a pumpkin without any of the complications. Beautiful orange Thai paper decoupaged onto a wire kitchen basket makes up the body. A tea light sits on an old can in the bottom of the basket, providing a delightful orange glow at a safe distance from the walls of the lantern. Another benefit of this pretend pumpkin? You can use it year after year.

YOU WILL NEED

1. Pierce a few holes in the bottom of a food can. Thread the thin wire through the holes to attach the can securely to the bottom of the basket. The can will safely hold a small tea light or votive candle.

2. Tear your paper into 1-inch-wide strips (2.54 cm). Tear the long strips into manageable lengths.

3. Pour the decoupage medium into a bowl. Thin it with a small amount of water.

4. Dip a single strip of paper in the medium. Lay the strip on the basket and smooth it into place. Don't fret if it looks as if it isn't sticking.

CLEAN PET FOOD CANS
WIRE KITCHEN BASKETS
THIN WIRE
AWL
THAI UNRYU PAPER*
BLACK TISSUE PAPER
DECOUPAGE MEDIUM
BOWL
BRUSH
PLASTIC SHEETING
TEA LIGHT OR VOTIVE CANDLE

*Tissue paper will work in a pinch, but the long fibers of the unryu paper work best.

Dip another strip in the medium. Overlap this strip with the previous strip. Continue adding strips until the top portion of the basket is covered. Let it dry overnight.

5. Once the basket is dry, turn it over and cover the bottom as you did in step 4. Let it dry.

6. Cut out tissue paper features. Use decoupage medium to adhere them to the lantern.

7. Give the lantern a final coat of decoupage medium. Let it dry.

8. Place a lit tea light or votive in the can.

Lantern by Terry Taylor

WITCH'S MUD ROOM

A witch's meeting is convened indoors, and all witches are asked to leave their hats and brooms at the door. This display presents the lighter side of witches. Their hats are playful rather than scary, and their brooms are actually quite beautiful. The witch hats (made from cardboard and papier-mâché) are oversized for impact. The brooms spend the rest of the year as part of a folk crafts collection, but at Halloween, they easily shift context into a witchy tablcau.

HALLOWEEN
BOO-TANICALS

Fresh flowers and greenery
are not the stuff of Halloween.
They're a little too, *optimistic*, don't
you think? Dried ferns with skeletal
branch formations make an eerie
but appealing arrangement.
Use witchy-looking vintage shoes
instead of a vase. The scene looks as
though some unfortunate witch fell
under a shape-shifting spell, leaving
only her boots beneath her as she
shrunk down into a fiddlehead fern.

If you're longing for some green
but still want something sinister,
how about a carnivorous plant?

Floral arrangement by Susan McBride

HEX DOLLS

On a dark Halloween night, you see something, or things, hanging from the front porch, swinging in the wind. You can't quite make out what it is, but as you get closer you discover that the mysterious objects are human-shaped stick figures, dangling threateningly above, sending out a cryptic but clearly ominous message.

What is it about these hex dolls that makes them so scary? Often the obscure is much more frightening than the obvious. The primitive look implies that these figures were assembled by an inexpert hand, perhaps a hideous crone hiding somewhere in the attic?

To make your own terrifying stick dolls, just collect interesting-looking sticks while you're out on a walk or raking your yard. Look for sticks with unusual features or bumps that could be interpreted as human facial or body features.

When you've got an assortment of sticks, bind them together at the center with hemp twine. Attach found objects such as beads, buttons, bottle caps, or any interesting rusted hardware to the twine. These dolls feature cobalt glass and beads positioned over what would be the heart.

Hang your hex dolls from tree branches around the yard, from your front porch, or over your door. Trick-or-treaters and other Halloween visitors will look at you a little funny as they approach your door, uncertain as to whether or not they should be *really* afraid of you.

Hex dolls by Susan McBride

VOODOO DOLL

Black cats and witches are meant to be scary, but they've become so commonplace that they've lost their edge. If you're looking for a fresh way to creep out those who come to your door, try a voodoo doll. There's something a little unsettling about voodoo dolls, perhaps because one can never be completely sure that their power isn't real. Don't let appearances fool you, though. This one is actually a positive voodoo doll, meant to bring prosperity to its maker.

YOU WILL NEED

OLD T-SHIRT
MARKER OR MARKER PEN
SEWING MACHINE AND THREAD
SCISSORS
OLD MAGAZINE
OLD DOLL (OPTIONAL)
RAFFIA (OPTIONAL)
RIBBONS (OPTIONAL)
FRINGE OR NETTING (OPTIONAL)
DRIED WEEDS OR STRAW (OPTIONAL)
LATEX WATER-BASED HOUSE PAINT, ANY COLOR
PAINTBRUSH
NEEDLE
HEAVY QUILTING THREAD
Any of the following embellishments: buttons, beads, metal washers, small toys, sequins, paper money, old cards, and photographs

Doll by Lois Simbach

1. Lay the T-shirt on a flat surface and draw a rough gingerbread man outline with the marker. Don't worry if the lines are not perfect; they will not be seen in the finished doll.

2. Cut the doll shape out of the shirt leaving about ¹/₂ inch (1.3 cm) of fabric around the doll, making sure you clip the curves.

3. Sew around the outline of the doll. Stretch the fabric as you sew so that the thread doesn't break when you stuff the doll. Leave about 2 inches (5.1 cm) open on the side so that you can insert the stuffing.

4. Reach inside the opening and turn the doll inside out so that the seams are hidden.

5. Tear out several pages from an old magazine. Lightly stuff the doll with crumpled magazine pages. Roll the magazine pages into tubes and crumple them to stuff in the arms and legs of the doll. You will want to keep the doll as lightweight as possible.

6. Cut the hair off of an old doll.

7. Fold the top open edges of the doll inward about 1 inch (2.5 cm) and stuff the old doll hair inside. Sew the hair into the top of the head using the zigzag seam on the sewing machine. You can also use raffia, ribbons, fringe, netting, dried weeds, or straw for your doll's hair.

8. Paint the doll using the dry brush method. Make sure that you don't soak the doll with paint or the stuffing will get wet. Don't use an oil-based paint as it will take too long to dry. You can paint your doll in a solid color, half one color and half another, or with polka dots, squiggles, and blotches.

9. Cut a male and female face out of the magazine and sew one to each side of your doll using a simple slipstitch.

10. Add button eyes, beads, and a metal washer for the mouth of your doll. Trace around the embellishments with a marker to emphasize them if you like.

11. To decorate the body area, sew small toys, words from the magazine, trinkets, sequins, paper money, old cards, and photographs on your doll. You can even devise a theme for your doll. Make sure that you double the heavy quilting thread when sewing on the charms so that your doll will be sturdy.

12. Sew a small, closed ring of the heavy quilting thread or ribbon at the hairline of your doll. This will allow your doll to dangle in the air, showing off both sides of your creation.

CORN DOLLY

You may have never seen or even heard of a corn dolly (an entirely different thing than a corn husk doll), but they've been made around Halloween for hundreds of years. European farmers always made a corn dolly at the end of each harvest to persuade the spirit of the corn to return the next year (see page 127 for more information). These modern, updated corn dollies by California artist Barbara Evans revive the tradition in an elegant, but edgy way. Corn dollies look great on a mantle, hanging from a front door, or as a table centerpiece at a fall gathering.

YOU WILL NEED

4-OUNCE (115 G) BUNDLE
OF NATURAL WHEAT*

WATER

RAFFIA

WIRE SNIPS

20-GAUGE WIRE

12-TO 14-INCH-TALL (30.5 TO 35.6 CM)
PAPER CONE, HEAVY PAPER, OR PAPER BAG

SCISSORS

GLUE

SMALL STRAIGHT PINS

CORNHUSKS*

*Available at craft stores

Corn Dolly by Barbara Evans

INSTRUCTIONS ARE FOR THE LARGE DOLL IN THE CENTER OF THE PHOTO.

1. Soak the wheat stalks in the water until they are pliable.

2. Sort the stalks, putting all those with short seed heads into a pile to be used for the hands of the doll, and those with long seed heads in a pile to be used for the head.

FOR THE HEAD

1. Start with one of the wheat stalks you selected for the head and center four more long-headed wheat stalks around it.

2. Tie the stalks together with a piece of the raffia.

3. Tie another row of six to seven long-headed wheat stalks at the base of the four joined stalks.

4. Continue repeating the process, adding several more stalks to each new row than were in the previous row. Your aim is to make a nicely shaped head for the doll. Five to six rows should suffice.

5. Wrap a piece of raffia around the base of the seed heads to create the neck.

FOR THE BODY

1. Use a paper cone, or if you don't have one, make one by trimming heavy paper or a paper bag to a 12-to 14-inch (30.5 to 35.6 cm) section, then roll the paper or the bag into a cone shape and glue it into place.

2. Put some glue on the tip of the paper cone and place the long stalks of the doll's body over it, spreading them out so that they are evenly spaced around the circumference of the cone.

All dolls by Barabara Evans

3. Wrap the wheat stalks with the raffia at the middle and the bottom of the paper cone.

FOR THE ARMS

1. Sort out seven to eight of the wheat stalks with short heads for each hand or arm. Make sure that the stems don't have any joints.

2. Tie the wheat bundles with the raffia just under the seed head to create the wrist.

3. Trim each bundle so that each arm is the length you want.

4. Cut four pieces of 20-gauge wire with wire snips. Each piece should equal the length of the stalks you trimmed for the arms.

5. Working very carefully, gently slide one of the pieces of wire into a wheat stalk and work it to where the wrist of the doll is tied. Repeat for the other arm. Trim the ends of the wire if needed.

6. Wrap the arms with raffia exactly in the center to hold them together. This wrap will be hidden inside the stalks coming down from the head.

7. Gently separate the wheat stalks just below the neck and insert the arms. The arms must be positioned before the wheat stalks and raffia dry.

8. Wrap and tie the neck and body stalks with the raffia just below the inserted arms to hold them securely in place.

9. Very gently bend the arms a little toward the front at the shoulders and then bend the elbows. If the stalks tend to separate at the elbows, tie them together temporarily with raffia until they dry.

FOR THE DRESS

1. Starting at the bottom of the cone, attach cornhusks to build the skirt up, layer by layer, using glue, tiny pins, and raffia to hold them in place. If needed, trim the cornhusks as you finish each layer (do this while the husks are still wet and flexible).

2. As you approach the top of the cone, stop layering and place two strips of cornhusks over the shoulders of the doll to make a dress bodice. Tie the cornhusks with raffia at the "waist." Put some glue on the knot at the back of waist tie before you tighten the knot.

Before modern science came along to explain the mysteries of nature, people in cultures around the world attributed the caprice of the elements and the success or failure of the harvest to the approval or displeasure of the gods and goddesses that ruled the natural world. Utterly dependent on staple crops such as wheat, oat, and barley for survival, ancients courted the favor of the spirit of the grain, always depicted as a woman, to ensure the bounty of the next harvest. The ancient Egyptians called her Isis, while the Greeks called her Demeter. Whatever her name, she appears in the belief systems of cultures around the world.

Through the centuries, various cultures developed different ways of honoring the grain goddess and entreating her help. At harvest time, festivals were held to ensure that, as winter approached and the fields lay fallow, the living spirit of the grain wouldn't abandon the fields but would return again the next year. In pre-Christian Europe, farmers believed that the grain goddess would come to inhabit the last sheaf harvested if they formed it into a female figure which could be preserved over the winter and returned to the field the next spring. This tradition continued after the spread of Christianity, despite its links to the pagan past. The creation of the Corn Dolly, as the figure is known in England, lost its spiritual significance but remained a widely practiced cultural tradition.

Although harvest celebrations vary from culture to culture and have altered through the centuries, the honor of creating the corn dolly was often given to the first farmer to finish reaping. After the last sheaf was cut and formed into a corn dolly, the figure was decorated, sometimes with ribbons, and carried on a wagon or pole back to the farmer's home. In some cultures, the figure was doused in water and ritual dances were performed in celebration. Holding a feast at the end of the harvest is a constant across cultures around the world. After winter had passed and the farmers once again took to the fields, the corn dolly was traditionally placed in the freshly plowed furrows so that the spirit of the grain would once again inhabit the fields.

While the term corn dolly is used, wheat, rye, oats, or barley were actually more common crops in Europe. Native American nations celebrated the maize harvest, while Mediterranean farmers rejoiced over the bounty of the vineyards.

While skill of making corn dollies was passed down through the generations, modern technology almost brought an end to this ancient tradition. With the advent of large mechanical threshing machines, grain sheaves were damaged, leaving none intact. People began celebrating the harvest in church rather than in family homes, and many quit farming and moved into cities. The tradition of making corn dollies had almost disappeared entirely until it was revived in recent decades. Although the rituals associated with creating corn dollies may no longer be performed, the figures themselves remain as a link to the ancient understanding of the link between man and nature.

ALONG CAME A SPIDER

When it comes to outdoor Halloween decorations, scale is everything. A collection of tiny spiders hanging from a front porch is mildly creepy. A gigantic spider taking up the entire front yard is downright dazzling in a slightly unsettling way. This squatting spider looks like she's sitting on a nest that's about to burst, releasing thousands of baby spiders all over the neighborhood. She's made of weatherproof outdoor carpeting and landscape fabric, so she can take up residence on your grass and survive the elements indefinitely.

YOU WILL NEED

BLACK SYNTHETIC INDOOR-OUTDOOR CARPETING*

STRONG SCISSORS

HOT GLUE GUN AND GLUE STICKS

LANDSCAPE FABRIC

LAWN AND GARDEN TRASH BAGS

FALLEN LEAVES (OPTIONAL)

FOAM PIPE INSULATION**

HEAVY-GAUGE WIRE

PLIERS OR WIRE CUTTERS

BATTERY-OPERATED ROUND PUSH LIGHTS**

*This material is usually sold at hardware stores in 6-to 10-foot (1.8 to 3 m) widths.
**Available at home improvement or hardware stores.

Spider by Trulee Grace Hall

SEASONAL SILHOUETTES

If the spiderweb-in-the-windowsill trick has lost its appeal for you, try a sophisticated alternative to window dressing. Find a copyright-free image that you like and copy it onto a sheet of vellum, adjusting the size to fit your window. We used a variety of images, from the spooky bat and skeleton to the charming acorn or moon and stars. Simply cut around the image so that it fits in your windowpane and tape it in place. Since vellum is translucent, your silhouettes won't block the light coming through the window. We arranged several silhouettes in diagonals to complement the pattern of the windows. This is a fast, easy, and inexpensive way to add Halloween atmosphere to your home.

See page 170 for templates or make up your own seasonal silhouettes.

1. Decide how large you'd like your spider to be. Measure out enough synthetic carpeting to make the spider's "hump." Cut a circle from the material (for our spider, the circle was 6 feet [1.8 m] in diameter). Cut another, smaller circle from landscape fabric for the spider's underbelly.

2. Hot glue the hump to the underbelly, leaving about 1 foot (30.4 cm) open so that you can stuff the spider.

3. Stuff the spider with raked leaves, recycled lawn and garden bags, or whatever else might be practical and weather-resistant.

4. You will need eight hollow tubes of foam pipe insulation for the spider's legs. Measure out and cut the tubes to an appropriate length for the

spider's legs. They should be proportionate to the body and long enough to stretch up and out for a dramatic presentation.

5. You'll cover the foam legs with landscape fabric. Double the length measurement you took for the legs, then cut a piece of landscape fabric to this measurement for each leg. The width should be wide enough to fit loosely around the leg (about 6 to 10 inches [15.2 to 25.4 cm] wide).

6. Center one of the tube legs on top of one of the landscape fabric strips. Fold the strip around the leg and hot glue the long edges together, making sure you don't glue the fabric cover to the tube leg (you want it to be loose). Bunch up the fabric on the tube leg, and then hot glue the short ends of the fabric cover to the tube legs.

7. Cut eight pieces of heavy-gauge wire to the length of the legs. Insert the wire into the hollow center of each tube, allowing it to extend beyond the leg about 4 inches (10.2 cm) on one end of each tube. Decide on the position of your legs (the wire should be flexible enough so that you can bend the legs up or out). Poke one end of the wire into the hump to attach the leg.

8. The last detail is the eyes. Give your spider a look of its own by personalizing its expression. Two round push lights were used for glowing eyes. For our spider, slanted eye shapes were painted on top of the lights to create a sinister look. Glue a little loop of wire to the back of the plastic lights and sew or wire them into place.

MENACE of the PUMPKIN PATCH

This scarecrow definitely isn't smiling. In fact, he doesn't even have a mouth. Looming over the garden, his twisting, viney frame is poised to pounce on any who dare to pluck the bounty of the pumpkin patch without permission. A swift swipe from one of his pitchfork hands could spell disaster for unsuspecting humans.

If cheerful straw figures aren't your cup of tea, consider a slightly more sinister alternative. Artist and gardener Christopher Mello made this towering creature from scrap industrial reinforcement wire and a mass of vines from his garden.

He's about 10-feet (3 m) tall and very flexible, which gives him a hulking appearance. Mello first built the wire frame, then wrapped the vines around it. The hands and feet are made from discarded pitchforks, attached to the central wire and vines with wire twisted around the "wrists." Rusted metal scraps circle the center of the body to give the illusion of a waist. A long metal stake is attached to one leg and can be driven into the ground so that the creature can stand up. The pumpkin "head" is stuck through a wire at the top of the frame. No features were carved on the head, which actually contributes to its scariness.

Use this figure as inspiration for your own creation that puts the scare back in scarecrow.

Figure by Christopher Mello

CROP CIRCLE LUMINARIA

Could there be anything eerier that crop circles? They are giant cryptic designs, sometimes miles long, mysteriously cut into grain fields under cover of darkness. The patterns are so huge that they can only be seen from an airplane and so fanatically executed that the process seems beyond human capability. On Halloween night, crop circle designs are a delightfully different choice for luminaria.

1. Choose the pictures of crop circle designs that have circles and straight lines. You want an interesting design, but if too many holes in the bag connect, it won't be stable. Use the templates on page 170 as a guide.

2. Trim the cutting mat or a piece of cardboard to fit inside the paper bags. This will keep you from cutting through both sides of the paper bags. Slide the mat into one of the paper bags carefully and so that the inside folds of the paper bag are protected as well.

3. Trace your crop circle design onto the bag. To cut the design with a circle cutter, follow the manufacturer's instructions. In designs with circles within circles, leave some paper to link the circles together in at least two places. When cutting a circle and leaving links in the paper, don't worry about getting to the exact point of the link with the circle cutter. You can cover the details with the craft knife later.

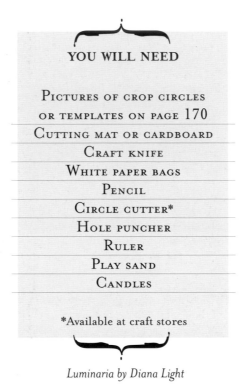

YOU WILL NEED

PICTURES OF CROP CIRCLES
OR TEMPLATES ON PAGE 170

CUTTING MAT OR CARDBOARD

CRAFT KNIFE

WHITE PAPER BAGS

PENCIL

CIRCLE CUTTER*

HOLE PUNCHER

RULER

PLAY SAND

CANDLES

*Available at craft stores

Luminaria by Diana Light

They're HERE...

Safety note: Make sure you keep enough of the sides of the bag intact so that there are no edges there that could accidentally catch on fire. As always when working with fire, make sure to monitor the lit candles carefully.

4. Use a hole punch to create small circles. The circle cutter will only go 1 inch (2.5 cm) in diameter at the smallest setting.

5. Use the craft knife and a ruler to cut the straight lines.

6. When you are finished with your design, put some sand in the bottom of the bag. Place a candle in the bag, lodging the bottom straight in the sand so that it holds up firmly.

7. For maximum effect, put the luminaria near a wall so that the shadow from your crop circle projects up onto it.

Templates for crop circle designs appear on page 170.

HALLOWEEN CANDLESCAPING

Create a gentle orange glow over your fireplace, even if it's still too warm to make a fire. Tea lights in glass votive holders hidden behind mini-pumpkins bathe a room in a warm and inviting light. Add lanterns for a charming seasonal tableau.

Mini-pumpkins float, and when interspersed with candles and fall flowers in a beautiful glass bowl, they make an elegant table or front porch display.

Tabletop
Victorian Graveyard

Nothing says spooky like Victorian gravestones.
Bring a whole graveyard full of them into your
home and place them on your mantle for some
Halloween seasonal spirit that's ghostly, but not
ghastly. Scour copyright-free clip art books or
web sites for images of obelisks, tombs, weeping
angels, and mausoleums. Enlarge or reduce the
images on a copy machine. Mount the images on
foam-core board with an adhesive spray and cut
them out with a sharp craft knife. Cut small triangles out of the leftover board. Glue the triangles to the reverse of the mounted images to
make them stand. Arrange your mini-cemetery
on a tabletop or mantel with a few votive candles
hidden behind the tombs.

Figures by Terry Taylor

Jack-o'lanterns aren't your only option for glowing light on Halloween. Purchase pumpkin-shaped candles for elegant tabletop displays.

Black tapers in a spindly candelabra give you lots of spooky atmosphere.

Parties

When it comes to parties, consider the timeless advice of a famed socialite. Consoling a young protégé who lamented an appalling lack of parties to attend, the doyenne counseled, "Darling, you have to *make* the occasion." As Halloween approaches, keep this sage advice in mind. If you find yourself in need of entertainment, but your mailbox yields no invitations, take matters into your own hands and host your own unforgettable Halloween fête.

A Halloween party may conjure up all sorts of images: bobbing for apples, caramel popcorn balls, a bowl of green punch garnished with a floating plastic severed hand. There is a time and a place for those old standbys, but a Halloween party doesn't have to be ghoulish, and fake blood is not a prerequisite for having a good time. Why not try a party with a little more flair?

We've assembled a stylish trio of party ideas for All Hallows' Eve, all a little bit spooky, yet sophisticated.

Try a cocktail party with a New Orleans voodoo theme, a Day of the Dead party with delicious Mexican fare, or a Masked Ball and dessert soiree. We provide ideas for invitations, activities, recipes, and ambience. Your party needn't be big and lavish —just assemble a few guests committed to an otherworldly evening of entertainment and a memorable Halloween night.

New Orleans Voodoo
Cocktail Party

For a Halloween night full of bayou black magic, host a New Orleans-style voodoo cocktail party. Conjure up the ambience of New Orleans' French Quarter, sometime in the not-too-distant past, a place where the mystery of voodoo hangs in the air and you never know what's going on in the rooms behind the lace-iron balconies. Think sultry nights and whirling ceiling fans, candles, tarot cards, and thick red brocade curtains from behind which a black-gloved hand beckons you. This intriguing setting is the perfect backdrop for a stylishly spooky cocktail party.

INVITATION

Your guests will have a hard time saying no to this intriguing invitation. Fill a red envelope with items evocative of voodoo, such as a handmade voodoo doll, candles, and incense. Write the party particulars on a parchment paper scroll, and roll it up in the envelope. If you don't have time to make a voodoo doll for each guest, you can always draw one or print out an image of one as a substitute.

VOODOO DOLL

Place a stick in the middle of a fabric scrap. Spread a small bunch of moss along the length of the stick so that a little is hanging over the edges, then roll the fabric around the moss and stick tightly, leaving one edge open.

Hot glue the fabric down on one edge. Fold another piece of fabric and wrap it around the top of the doll. Glue it down with hot glue. This will be the doll's head. Stuff moss into the head and let it hang out of the top of the doll. Add a couple of feathers, pushing the ends down into the doll's head.

To make arms, poke a hole through the side of the doll approximately three-fourths of the way to the top of the body. Push the smaller stick through the hole in the fabric, working it through the moss and out a hole on the opposite side. Tie and knot small lengths of string along the bottom and middle sections of the doll. Do the same at the top and bottom edge of the head section. This gives the doll a little more of a human shape. Finish the doll by slipping a couple of pins through the body.

YOU WILL NEED

Fabric scrap
String
Spanish moss
2 small sticks (one slightly smaller than the other)
Feathers
Pins
Scissors
Craft glue
Craft brush
Hot glue gun and glue sticks
Oversized envelopes

CANDLES

Use small tapers and bind them together with corrugated cardboard or decorative paper.

INCENSE

Roll a few sticks of incense in a length of unbleached parchment or ordinary waxed paper. The parchment or waxed paper protects the rest of the envelope's contents from the oils in the incense.

INVITATION SCROLL

Write your invitation on a piece of white paper and roll it up in a small scroll. Tie with string. If you would like an aged look, either add some sepia-toned ink to the edges of the paper or (carefully!) burn the edges.

ENVELOPE

Find a sufficiently large envelope and fill it with the objects.

If you plan to mail this invitation rather than hand deliver it, write HAND CANCEL along the side to protect the contents.

Invitation by Nicole Tuggle

AMBIENCE

You and your guests can wear costumes or opt out of them. The early nineteenth century was the heyday of voodoo in New Orleans, so you might want to turn to that period for inspiration. Regency-style dresses in red or black with black lace, like the one on page 55, are just right. For gentlemen, think riverboat gamblers or zombies.

To create a creepy bayou atmosphere, drape everything in sight in Spanish moss (you can buy it at craft stores). For lighting, use candles, candles, candles—as many as you can without causing a fire hazard. Red is a powerful color in voodoo, so use red candles if you can find them. Find a spooky candelabra and let the wax drip over the arms for an eerie effect. Incense is key—you'll want the air to be thick with it.

Create a spooky tableau with bones, feathers, or animal horns. String red hot peppers around—they're often used in voodoo spells. It *is* Halloween, after all, so leave a few small pumpkins and gourds around to remind everyone.

Since this is a cocktail party, you don't need to go overboard with food. New Orleans-style crawfish are a perfect solution if you can find them in your area (you can actually order them on-line for fresh delivery in just a few days). Make some infused oils, create a spooky name label for them, then tie them with black ribbon. You can use the oils on bread or in a salad, and your guests can take the remaining bottles home with them at the end of the evening.

To capture the spirit of New Orleans, play New Orleans blues. You'll find that a lot of the lyrics actually make reference to voodoo or hoodoo. An old recording of a great French chanteuse like Edith Piaf will help create a hauntingly chic atmosphere.

LIBATIONS

At your voodoo cocktail party, your guests will certainly expect to find the libation most commonly associated with voodoo, the Zombie. You may also want to try another concoction strongly associated with New Orleans, the Hurricane. Both are powerful brews, so advise your guests to exercise restraint—a single one of these drinks per guest is a good rule of thumb. You should also provide some options for the nondrinking guest. A delicious Planter's Punch "mocktail" is the perfect choice for this party.

ZOMBIE

1 ounce (29.5 ml) light rum
1 ounce (29.5 ml) dark rum
¼ ounce (7.3 ml) 151 proof rum
½ ounce (14.7 ml)
apricot brandy
1 ounce (29.5 ml) pineapple juice
1 ounce (29.5 ml) lime juice
2 ounces (59 ml) orange juice
1 cup (198 g) crushed ice
1 teaspoon (5 g) superfine sugar

Shake in a cocktail shaker if you have one. If not, blend with a stirrer or in a blender at low speed. Pour into a Tom Collins glass and garnish with mint sprigs, a cherry, or orange peels. It's acceptable to drink this cocktail with a straw, if desired.

PLANTER'S PUNCH MOCKTAIL

3 ounces (88.7 ml) orange juice
1 ounce (29.5 ml) lime juice
1 teaspoon (4.9 ml)
passion fruit syrup
Dash of grenadine
Dash of Angostura bitters

Blend in an Irish coffee glass or Tom Collins glass. Garnish with an orange slice.

HURRICANE COCKTAIL

1 ounce (29.5 ml) dark rum
1 ounce (29.5 ml) light rum
½ ounce (14.7 ml) lime juice
½ ounce passion fruit syrup
or grenadine

Shake in a cocktail shaker or blend well with a spoon or stirrer. Pour into a big brandy glass and garnish with a lime or orange peels. You can also drink this cocktail with a straw.

The items in a gris-gris bag are gathered for specific purposes, such as attracting love, luck, or money, or protecting against evil. Gris-gris bags must contain an odd number of items, but never more than 13: three, five, and seven items are the most common amounts. The items in a bag depend its purpose: charms, candles, incense, roots, herbs, oils, feathers, coins, lodestones, bones, nuts, and personal items are often used for "spells." Some say that a bag should contain something from each of the four elements: earth, air, fire, and water (salt, incense, oil, and a candle would do it). Uncommon items, often thought to be more powerful, include such things as graveyard dust, shark's teeth, bat wings, cat's hair, or dove's blood mixed with pine tree sap. Red flannel bags are the most common types of bags used, but other colors are used for specific purposes: green for money, blue for peace, white for babies.

PARTY FAVOR

Give your guests a lasting reminder of your voodoo soiree by giving each one a mock gris-gris bag. A gris-gris bag (also known as conjure bag, mojo bag, mojo hand, root bag, toby, nation sack, or wanga bag) is a small pouch containing items believed to work magic.

The root doctor or conjure woman (also known as voodoo queen) who assembles or "dresses" a bag, "smokes" it with incense or pours liquid (such as alcohol or bodily fluids) on it to activate it. If the bag is meant for good purposes, such as attracting love or money, the user would wear the bag under his or her clothing (women carry the bag on their left side, men to the right). If the bag is meant to "put a gris-gris" or curse on someone, it could be thrown at the unfortunate recipient or put under his doorstep or pillow. Finding a gris-gris bag is considered bag luck and means that you'd better watch out.

To make a gris-gris bag just for fun, assemble some interesting items in a bag and let each guest choose his or her own bag. You can make up your own "recipes" or use the ones in the following list.

HOODOO GRIS-GRIS BAG RECIPES *from* LOUISIANA

Love Come to Me	Good Luck	Money	Protection
Red bag	Green bag	Green flannel bag	White candles
Red or pink candle	Cinnamon	Coin	Oil (enough for 9 days)
Red feather	Basil	A pinch of sugar	Tiger's eye
Red thread	Sugar	Lodestone	Carnation petals
2 lodestones	Alligator tooth	Charm	Star anise
Rosebud	Charm	John-the-Conqueror-root	Turquoise
Lemon peel			Camphor
Shell			

GLOSSARY

CHARM. An item that has special powers, such a chicken bone, a lodestone, or a coin.

GRIS-GRIS BAG (see page 146). Bag containing charms or talismans used in casting spells. Also called mojo bag.

HOODOO. Considered to be the folk magic branch of voodoo, hoodoo focuses on herbs, healing practices, and spells. Most of the symbols commonly associated with voodoo (dolls, bags, potions, herbs, oils, etc.) are actually used in hoodoo, not voodoo. Slaves or former slaves who came to the United States from what is now Haiti developed hoodoo in southern Louisiana.

HOUNGAN. Male voodoo priests, who tell the future, casts spells, and create potions.

JU-JU. Fetish doll or sacred object. Said to be needed by a witch doctor to make magic work, be it good or evil.

LOA. The spirits of all things that live in the universe. Voodoo believers honor hundreds of loa who control nature, health, wealth, and happiness. During voodoo ceremonies, loa are said to possess or *ride* the participants to give them guidance and warnings.

MAMBO. Female voodoo priestess.

MOJO. See gris-gris bag. The word mojo comes from the west African word mojuba, which means prayer or homage. Mojo is used most commonly to describe the bag which contains items used for a spell.

SANTERIA. Another African-based religion which developed in Cuba. Like voodoo, Santeria blends traditional African beliefs with elements of Catholicism. On other Caribbean islands, similar religions developed. Obeah is a Jamaican form of Voodoo, and Shango is the folk religion practiced in Trinidad.

VOODOO (also voodun, voduoiu, vaudoun). A belief system with roots in traditional African belief systems and Catholicism. Voodoo developed in the Caribbean as slaves brought there by French colonists blended their own beliefs with those imposed on them by the colonists. One of the core beliefs of voodoo is that everything in the universe is interconnected—humans and nature, the living and the dead. In voodoo, objects and natural phenomena are believed to have souls which possess or "ride" voodoo believers during ceremonies in order to impart wisdom or give them messages. Drums and dancing are an essential part of voodoo services. Black magic is a very minor aspect of voodoo.

ZOMBIE. Zombie is the term used for the living dead, a human who is poisoned by a bokor (male priest who practices black magic) and then comes back to life without a soul to serve him as a mindless but strong slave. Some speculate that zombies were actually people under the influence of a natural herbal narcotic that turned them into semiconscious beings. Primarily the zombie was a belief in Haitian Voodoo; however Marie Laveau's snake was named Li Grand Zombi.

ACTIVITY:
TAROT READING

Divination games aimed at predicting the future were the highlight of any Victorian Halloween party. Young women played games with apples or hazelnuts, hoping to discover their romantic fate. Playing cards, and specifically tarot cards, have also been used historically to look into the future. Despite their reputation for predicting gloom and doom, tarot cards aren't the menacing oracles of the occult they're often portrayed to be. Halloween can be a good opportunity to learn more about them, and since they're often associated with voodoo, a tarot reading might be a fun party activity.

Tarot cards were invented in Italy sometime in the fifteenth century. They started out as ordinary playing cards, with no deeper meaning than the standard playing cards that we use today. There were numbered cards, royal suites, and cards with symbols such as the Emperor, the Pope, Death, the Devil, and the Moon. Some of the images may seem macabre to the modern viewer, but they were commonly recognized symbols in the Middle Ages and didn't have a sinister meaning. A game called the Game of Triumphs (similar to bridge) was played with the cards, and it became a popular game among the upper classes throughout Europe.

As the centuries passed, cardmakers and artists reinterpreted the images on the cards. Sometime around the late eighteenth century, the cards came to be associated with divination and the occult, and people began to see mystical meaning in the symbols of the cards. Around the same time, the symbols on the cards started to change dramatically to reflect the new interpretation of their meaning.

There is no definitive version of the tarot deck—different symbols appear in different decks, and different meanings are ascribed to each card. Most commercially sold tarot decks come with a how-to book. You can also find on-line courses and dozens of books on the subject if you're interested in teaching yourself how to read the cards.

Typically, a reading starts with shuffling the cards, asking a question, placing the cards face down, and drawing cards. To determine the answer, the reader creates a "spread" of one to three cards, laying the cards out in the order that they were drawn. Each card will indicate a part of the answer to the question. In one interpretation of a three-card spread, the first card represents the past, the second the present, and the third the future.

Tarot reading can be a fun Halloween party activity, even if there's no expert on hand to interpret the cards. It's an interesting way to learn about the cards and their history.

MARIE LAVEAU:
The Voodoo Queen

In New Orleans, a city with a long history of colorful characters, perhaps the most memorable is Marie Laveau, the renowned *voodooienne*, or voodoo queen. Respected and feared from the top echelons of power to the homes of slaves, she was said to be able to predict the future, cast and remove spells, concoct love potions, and impose curses. More than a century after her death, she still casts a long shadow in New Orleans history.

New Orleans in the 1830s was a fascinating melange of cultures, full of intrigue and secrecy—the perfect atmosphere for the birth of a legend. Here at the mouth of the Mississippi River, pirates, smugglers, gamblers, displaced European aristocrats, and opportunistic adventurers from the new United States all gathered to seek their fortunes, often in a less than legal manner. Stories of New Orleans from this time sizzle with drama: duels, poisoned enemies, shady characters, and mysterious disappearances were the order of the day.

Onto this dramatic backdrop, enter Marie Laveau. Her rise to fame has all the elements of a great legend.

According to the most famous story about her (part of which can be authenticated through historical documents), Laveau, a hairdresser to elite New Orleanian women, gained her acclaim as a voodoo priestess through a well-publicized court victory. A wealthy Creole man who had heard of her success in black magic entreated her to help his son to beat a murder charge. The next day Madam Laveau reportedly spent the morning praying in St. Louis cathedral with three guinea peppers in her mouth, then went to the courthouse and hid them under the judge's chair. When the verdict was read later in the day, the boy was found innocent, against all odds.

What was the secret of her success? Was it voodoo or something else?

Although misunderstanding about voodoo led to wild speculation among New Orleans' white population (voodoo followers were said to drink the blood of roosters and sacrifice black cats), the voodoo Marie Laveau practiced focused mostly on prayers for healing and good fortune. Spells, potions, voodoo dolls, curses, and so-called "black magic," were only a small part of voodoo beliefs.

The real source of Laveau's power it seems came not from magic but from her shrewd use and manipulation of information. As a hairdresser, she had discovered that the city's wealthy women used the styling chair as confessional. Infidelity, political intrigue, financial impropriety, and illness were all revealed to Laveau, who later used the information, either through blackmail or through the power of suggestion. Knowing that servants and slaves were the eyes and ears of a wealthy household, she developed a network of spies who would collect information from the elite and pass it on to her for her use.

To press servants into her service, Madam Laveau was said to convince them that they were under a voodoo curse. She would leave a voodoo doll near a servant's door, and when that person came to her for help, she would offer to lift the curse in exchange for information about his or her boss. Laveau used the information to combat her clients' enemies, protect them from harm, bring lovers together, or tear them apart. She could reportedly even rig an election. Her victory in the renowned court case was seemingly not due to the placement of the guinea peppers but to her manipulation of a witness.

Like so many powerful women, Laveau was a complicated figure, full of contradictions. She was a mother of 15 children and attended church every day. She helped the American wounded at the Battle of New Orleans and aided the city's prominent citizens with potions during the Yellow Fever epidemic of the 1850s. Then again, she's said to have run a bordello on New Orleans' lakefront, using the women to gain secrets from the city's most powerful men. The truth about her has mostly been replaced by legend.

To this day, tourists to New Orleans still visit the reported site of Laveau's grave to leave offerings and ask favors from the celebrated Voodoo Queen.

Day of the Dead
Dinner Party

In Mexico, the last day of October sees homes and public squares festooned not in orange and black, but bright pink, purple, and white, the colors of El *Día de Los Muertos*, the Day of the Dead, which is celebrated on November 1. This Halloween, instead of subjecting your guests to gastronomically gory fare like eyeball stew and brain-shaped gelatin molds, why not host a Day of the Dead dinner party? It's a great opportunity to explore a different cultural tradition and sample some delicious Mexican cuisine.

WHAT IS THE DAY *of the* DEAD?

Although Halloween and *El Día de Los Muertos* are celebrated at the same time of year, and skeletons are prominent symbols of both holidays, people often mistakenly assume that the Day of the Dead is just a Mexican version of Halloween. The two holidays do have some aspects in common—both trace their origins back thousands of years, and both were transformed with the spread of Christianity. While Halloween evolved from the Celtic holiday Samhain, the Day of the Dead sprang from pre-Columbian Mesoamerican festivals that celebrated departed ancestors. Just as Samhain was replaced with the holy days All Saints' Day and All Souls' Day (and later, the secular holiday Halloween), the ancient Aztec and Toltec harvest festivals (traditionally celebrated in late summer) were replaced with the Day of the Dead, also celebrated on All Saints' and All Souls' Days.

But the similarity between the two holidays ends there. While Halloween emphasizes fear of otherworldy creatures and the ghoulish aspects of the afterlife, the Day of the Dead honors the cycle of life and recognizes that death is a part of it. The Day of the Dead is a joyful family event that celebrates departed ancestors and welcomes them back to the world of the living for a yearly visit. The skeletons so widely associated with the holiday are happy, not scary. They represent the dead doing the things they enjoyed while they were living.

The Day of the Dead is celebrated on two days: November 1 and 2. While traditions vary in different parts of Mexico, there are some general commonalities. On November 1, families celebrate *los angelitos* (the little angels), the spirits of departed children. On November 2, deceased adults are honored. On both days, families go to the gravesites of their relatives to decorate and renovate graves. They bring picnic lunches, flowers, and candles. The cemeteries are crowded with families, mariachi bands play festive music, and at night there are fireworks in some parts of Mexico.

The most important ritual of this holiday is the preparation of the family altar, or *ofrenda*, the centerpiece of the celebration. The altar is meant as a welcoming place for spirits to rest after their long journey back from the dead. On the evening of October 31, families begin to set up their altars with offerings for the returning spirits.

Tabletop altars in homes feature photos of the deceased, candles to light their way home, incense, flowers (especially marigolds), fruit, and lots of special food and beverages. A glass of water is provided for the thirsty traveling spirit. There may also be beer, tequila, or a traditional beverage called *atole*, which has been made in Central America for thousands of years.

Families prepare food for the dead, taking care to include dishes they enjoyed when they were alive. There may be simple food like rice and beans, sweet potatoes, and tortillas, or specialty items like mole.

Every family is sure to include *a pan de muerto,* or bread of the dead, on the altar. Different types of pan de muerto are made in different parts of Mexico, ranging from a round bread decorated with pink sugar and cross bones to a bone-shaped loaf. In some regions, a plastic skeleton is baked into the bread to bring good luck to the person who finds it. The dead are said to inhale the essence of the food rather than eating it. At the end of the holiday, leftover food is eaten by the living.

Altars also feature colorful decorations, such as *calaveras de dulce* (also known as *alfeñiques*) or sugar skulls. The skulls or other shapes, such as lambs or donkeys, are inscribed with the names of the dead and are decorated with colorful icing and tin foil. Toy coffins and whimsical skeletons called *calacas* also decorate homes and altars, and brightly colored paper cutouts and streamers called *papel picado* hang from the ceilings and are strung up in public squares.

In addition to family events, some villages host parades of the dead. Skeleton figures dressed as a bride and groom lead the parade. People dressed as ghosts or skeletons, or in dark robes, march down the main street carrying an open coffin complete with a faux corpse. Spectators throw oranges, flowers, and candy into the coffin and at the "lucky corpse," who rolls his eyes and waves to the crowd as the procession winds its way to the cemetery. Masks also play a key role in the Day of the Dead. Skull masks are worn to public events, including ritual dances in public squares.

INVITATION

The bright marigold-colored paper used for these invitations is the first clue you'll give guests that your Halloween party is out of the ordinary.

Embellish the borders of the envelope with Mexican-inspired patterns. The ones on this envelope were created with a black and white photocopy transfer technique.

Find a decorative image you like and photocopy a section of it, reducing or enlarging it to fit on the border of your envelope. Lay the image face down on the envelope, then paint a thin layer of citrus stripper (a furniture refinishing product) or lacquer thinner onto the back of the photocopy. Citrus stripper is supposed to be safe to use indoors because the fumes aren't strong, but you must work outside or in a very well-ventilated area if you use lacquer thinner.

Rub the back of the photocopy with a wooden spoon, making sure you cover the whole area. Lift the paper, and your image should have transferred to the envelope. Use this process to transfer designs to the inside borders of the invitation as well.

The skeleton image is also a photocopier transfer cut out and attached to an accordion-pleated strip of paper so that it pops up off the page. Use rubber stamps to write out *Dia de Los Muertos* on the invitation, then write out the particulars about your party.

Invitation by Nicole Tuggle

AMBIENCE

The Day of the Dead is a festive holiday, so you want a festive atmosphere for
your party. String colorful paper garlands or papel picado (Mexican paper cutouts)
around the party area and the table to fill the room with color. A sombrero
makes a great centerpiece for your dinner table. You can put bowls of salsa
or other dips inside the wide brim. Sprinkle marigolds on the table and
use tall votive candles to add height to the display.

Costumes aren't necessary for this party, but great Mexican-inspired masks add to the fun. Skeleton masks are often worn for Day of the Dead celebrations. This horned mask combines the plaster mask technique described on page 96 with the technique for making horns on page 58. It's easy to find copyright-free images of La Catrina, the first lady of Day of the Dead, so she's a good choice if you're going to make a photocopy mask (see page 98).

The *ofrenda*, or altar, is the center-piece of your party. Select a corner of your room (or in this case, front porch) for a display with marigolds, fruit, corn, sugar skulls, and incense. Include candy or cookies like these ones decorated with skeletons for *los angelitos*, or little angels. Add something for the grown-up spirits to eat, too, such as red peppers or tortillas. Orange, yellow, or purple candles should light the altar. Use Mexican tin candleholders like these ones if you can find them. Authentic Day of the Dead altars always prominently feature antique photographs of ancestors or deceased relatives.

Make paper bag luminaria featuring copyright-free images of *calacas*, or Day of the Dead skeletons. We transferred the images to orange paper bags with a simple photocopy transfer technique (see page 153 for instructions).

This is a dinner party, so your guests will be expecting some fantastic Mexican fare. Mole, a spicy chocolate sauce, is a specialty on the Day of the Dead. Offer your guests a choice of soft drinks, Mexican beer, and margaritas, with or without alcohol. Make a pan de muerto with the recipe provided on page 156 or buy one from a Mexican bakery if you live near one.

Mexican music is infectiously upbeat, so make sure you have some playing in the background.

Mask top left by Ambra Lowenstein

FEASTING

PAN DE MUERTO

No Day of the Dead celebration would be complete without a *pan de muerto*, or bread of the dead. There are said to be over 200 different regional varieties of this sweet bread that is always found on family altars for the holiday.

The most common type of pan de muerto is round or oval, but some are bone or skull-shaped, and some look like angels, humans, or animals (especially rabbits). Sometimes extra strips of dough are attached to the side or top of the loaf so that it resembles a skeleton. The loaves are often decorated with sugar on top, and sometimes a plastic skeleton is baked inside the bread to bring luck to the person who finds it. Anise seed is a very common ingredient. Here's an easy pan de muerto recipe that makes enough bread for about 10 guests.

1. In a saucepan over medium flame, heat the butter, milk, and water until very warm, but not boiling.

2. Measure out 1½ cups (300 g) of flour and set the rest aside. In a large mixing bowl, combine the 1½ (300 g) cups of flour with the yeast, salt, anise seed, and sugar. Beat in the mixture you made in step 1 until well combined.

3. Add the eggs and beat in 1 cup (200 g) of flour. Continue adding more flour until dough is soft but not sticky.

Mask by Ambra Lowenstein

YOU WILL NEED

½ cup (100 g) butter
½ cup (103.5 ml) milk
½ cup (103.5 ml) water
5 to 5½ (653 to 900 g) cups
flour
2 packages dry yeast
1 teaspoon (5 g) salt
1 tablespoon (15 g) whole anise
seed
½ cup (100 g) sugar
4 eggs
Saucepan
Measuring cups
Mixing bowl
Bread board
Large glass bowl
Plastic wrap
Pastry brush

4. Knead the batter on a lightly floured board for 10 minutes until smooth and elastic.

5. Lightly grease a bowl and place the dough in it. Cover it with plastic wrap and let the dough rise in a warm place until it has doubled in bulk (about 1½ hours).

6. Punch the dough down and shape it into loaves resembling skulls or skeletons, or simply make a round or oval loaves. Let the loaves rise for 1 hour.

7. Preheat the oven to 350°F (176°C). Bake the bread for 40 minutes, then remove and let cool.

FOR THE GLAZE

You will need ½ cup (100 g) sugar, ⅓ cup (65 g) fresh orange juice, and 2 tablespoons (30 g) grated orange zest.

Mix the ingredients in a bowl and heat them in a saucepot. Bring the mixture to a boil for 2 minutes, then apply it to the bread with a pastry brush. If desired, sprinkle powdered sugar on top while the glaze is still damp.

ACTIVITY: MAKING SUGAR SKULLS

Even if you and your guests don't make the skulls, decorating them can be great fun. Brightly colored icing and foil are used to create designs on the skulls, and the name of an honored deceased family member is written on the skull with icing.

This is a messy activity, so have lots of paper towels and a source of water for washing hands nearby. You may want to make the skulls yourself

Making and decorating sugar skulls is a traditional Day of the Dead activity that will add a festive flavor to your party. Sugar skulls are used on altars and on gravesites during the holiday to honor the deceased. You can make them with purchased molds or shape the sugar into skulls yourself. We've included instructions for hand-sculpted skulls.

ahead of time and let your guests decorate them. You can prepare icing in advance so that all your guests have to do is pick up an icing bag and start decorating.

Can you eat sugar skulls?
Technically, yes, but in reality most people don't. Even though they may look delicious, they're really just for decoration and aren't very tasty. If kept dry, they can last up to two years.

The following recipe is to make eight skulls. Adjust the measurements as necessary.

BOILED ICING

YOU WILL NEED

3 EGG WHITES*

1⅓ CUP (202 G) GRANULATED SUGAR

3 TABLESPOONS (44.3 ML) OF COLD WATER

¼ TEASPOON (1.2 G) CREAM OF TARTAR

METAL BOWL

SAUCEPAN

* You can use powdered egg whites if desired.

Combine the ingredients in a metal bowl. Place the bowl in a saucepan of simmering water and beat the mixture with an electric mixer on low speed for about 5 minutes. Increase the speed and beat until very thick, about 4 minutes more. Remove the bowl from the saucepan and continue beating until light and fluffy, about another 4 minutes.

FOR THE SKULLS

YOU WILL NEED

WHISK

SPOON

1 TABLESPOON (15 G) POWDERED EGG WHITE

¾ CUP (177 ML) WATER

1½ TEASPOON (7.3 mL) VANILLA EXTRACT

¼ CUP (59 ML) LIGHT CORN SYRUP

8 CUPS (1.7 K) POWDERED SUGAR

2 CUPS (400 G) CORNSTARCH

BAKING SHEET

PLASTIC CLING WRAP

1. To make the skulls, whisk the powdered egg white and water together until foamy. Add vanilla extract and corn syrup. Whisk until blended. Add the powdered sugar. Mix with a spoon until a firm paste forms.

2. Dust a baking sheet with 1 cup (200 g) of the cornstarch. Knead your sugar paste in the cornstarch for a few minutes until it becomes smooth. Roll the dough into a ball. Wrap it in plastic and refrigerate it until chilled.

3. Shape the dough into balls, each about the size of a small fist. Add cornstarch as needed prevent to sticking.

4. Use your hands to shape the ball into a skull. Create the eye sockets and nose by pressing with your thumbs. Allow the skull to dry completely (anywhere from eight to 48 hours).

TO DECORATE THE SKULLS

YOU WILL NEED

PASTRY BAGS AND TIPS

DISPOSABLE FREEZER BAG (OPTIONAL)

COLORFUL FOIL*

*Available from on-line sources

To spread the icing, use a pastry bag or make your own with a disposable freezer bag—just snip the corner so that the icing can squeeze through. Add 2 to 3 ounces (62 to 93 g) of icing to your bag (it should be no more than one quarter full). Squeeze to decorate. You can also just apply icing with your fingers, although this can be messy.

Cut your foil into crowns, crosses, eyes, hearts, or the shape of your choice. To adhere it to the skull, just pat it down on top of the wet icing.

In addition to icing and foil, you may decorate the skulls with feathers, beads, sequins, labels, wrappers, glitter, and found objects added on with glue.

Party Favor

MEXICAN HOT CHOCOLATE

On October 31, there's no denying it anymore: winter is here. As a party favor, give your guests a treat that they'll enjoy on those cold nights to come—a Mexican hot chocolate package.

Chocolate has been made in Central America since the time of the Mayas, and the Aztecs who came along later called it the "food of the gods." The Aztecs combined chocolate with honey, nuts, seeds, and spices to make chocolate beverages which were often part of important rituals. Chocolate was so important in Aztec culture that it was used as currency.

If you've ever tried Mexican hot chocolate, you know that it's truly a world-class beverage. What makes it so special? There's something about the blend of bitter chocolate mixed with sugar, cinnamon, and nuts that creates a deep, smooth, satisfying taste.

Along with the chocolate, usually sold in disks, give your guests a cone of Mexican brown sugar and a generous mug so that they'll have something to use once the chocolate is gone.

Masked Ball
Dessert Party

Most of the time, having a few friends over for a nice meal
and a few glasses of wine is the maximum effort a working
grown-up can expend on entertaining. But there comes a time
in everyone's life to go beyond the ordinary and host a truly
legendary party. Louis XIV had *le Bal du Roy* in 1668. Truman
Capote had his Black and White Ball in the 1960s.
A Halloween masked ball and dessert party could be yours.
Are you ready to give it a try?

To pull off this party, you'll have to be committed to a vision.
Frankenstein's monster and the mummy must be turned away
at the door. This is an elegant affair with a spooky edge, a party
that seems like the ghost of lavish balls of the past. Don't be
intimidated, though. There's very little cooking involved, and
the decorating requires very little expense and only an after-
noon of styling. With a little time to plan and some willing
guests, your party should be a smashing success.

INVITATION

Make it easy for your guests to get in the spirit of the ball. If you provide them with a mask in the invitation, there's no excuse for them to show up without one. The Baroque look of this invitation sets the stage for an intriguing night and helps to build anticipation for your fabulous party.

YOU WILL NEED

CLEAR-DRYING ADHESIVE OR GLUE
BONE FOLDER OR BUTTER KNIFE
ENVELOPE TEMPLATE ON PAGE 171
WRAPPING PAPER WITH LETTERING
OR COLOR COPY OF OLD LETTER
COOKING PARCHMENT (BLEACHED
OR UNBLEACHED)
SCISSORS
MASK TEMPLATE ON PAGE 171

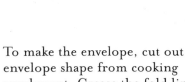

Invitation by Nicole Tuggle

To make the envelope, cut out envelope shape from cooking parchment. Crease the fold lines with a bone folder or butter knife. If using bleached parchment, place it on a baking sheet and bake it for 10 to 15 minutes at 325°F (162°C), and allow to cool. The paper will now have a light tan color. If you wish to age the envelopes further, smudge a light coat of sepia-toned ink along the edges.

Glue the envelope together with adhesive or glue, leaving the top flap open.

The invitation is written on a piece of wrapping paper that resembles an old hand-written letter. If you can't find paper like this, find an old letter in an antique store or copy one from a book. Color photocopy the letter onto stiff paper. Cut the letter to fit, writing side out, folded in

half inside your envelope. Write your invitation message by hand on the blank side of the letter, or drop a printed invitation inside.

Enlarge and photocopy the mask templates on page 171 onto thick paper. Cut along the outside edge, and place the mask, image side out, in the envelope over the old letter so it shows on the address side.

AMBIENCE

Your aim for this party is all-out opulence and an atmosphere that's a little ghostly. Remind your guests that this *is* a ball, so costumes are a must. Make it easy for them by including a mask base in the invitation (see page 171). All they need to do is decorate it—feathers, flowers, or collage are ideal materials. Your invitation phrasing should also encourage fancy dress. You may even want to include ideas on where they might find cast-off formal wear in your town. Since the eighteenth century was the golden age of masked balls, it's the perfect time period to emulate. Think Louis XIV, the Sun King, and Madam de Pompadour.

The fun part of preparing for this party is decorating. We chose a white, gold, and silver color scheme, reminiscent of a Versailles ball. Ghostly branches, painted white and strung with chandelier crystal "icicles," are elegant and eerie. Tulle is inexpensive, easy to find, and adds mystery to the atmosphere. Use it to drape your table and chairs, too. We ran minilights down the center of the table then added a layer of tulle on top. The effect is a subtly glowing table that invites guests to linger nearby. We snaked a white feather boa down the table and nested silver Christmas balls alongside it. The look is over-the-top and luxurious. Since this is a Halloween party, pumpkins and gourds play a part. Luckily, there are several varieties of white pumpkins and gourds. We even masked a few of them to echo the party theme.

Instead of flowers, which might be expensive or difficult to find at Halloween, we used white vases filled with dramatic plumes. These ones come from fall grasses, but you could also use feathers.

In terms of music, you may want to start the evening with some baroque music that's a little spooky. Harpsichord music has a haunting, Halloween feeling. Verdi's "Un Ballo a Maschera" is a must. If your guests are up for learning some baroque dance steps and you have the space, try a Viennese waltz by Strauss. As the night goes on, switch to something a little more upbeat. Lounge music from the 1950s might be just the ticket.

Silver and gold tableware are great choices for this party. You can add sparkly decorations to the handles of your trays to dress them up. Use a silver candelabra if you have one, with white candles, of course. If you can find them, vintage tea tins are great for displaying gourmet cookies. Just stuff the tin with silver tissue paper and artfully arrange the cookies inside. You can even tuck silvery decorations among the cookies for added sparkle. Glitter-covered plastic fruits are great in a centerpiece, or you can make real sugared fruit for an inviting display.

Treat your guests to a sumptuous dessert spread. Gourmet cookies and hard candies should spill from the trays. Make traditional Halloween desserts (didn't know there were such things?) from the recipes on page 167 to 168. We also provide a tempting punch recipe.

FEATHERED FANTASY MASKS

These incredible masks by Danusia Brandstetter are truly breathtaking. The feminine white one is made from parrot, ostrich, rooster, and goose feathers, with a white peacock quill and Czech crystal and other beads as accents. The masculine mask is made from golden pheasant, Reeve's pheasant, ringneck pheasant, rooster, and peacock feathers. The small deer antlers give it an otherworldly feel.

While you may not be able to re-create these masks (Danusia is an expert), don't be intimidated. Use a pre-made mask form as a base and add feathers (you can get them at craft stores or on-line) starting with the largest ones on the edge of the mask, working inward toward the eye holes with smaller feathers.

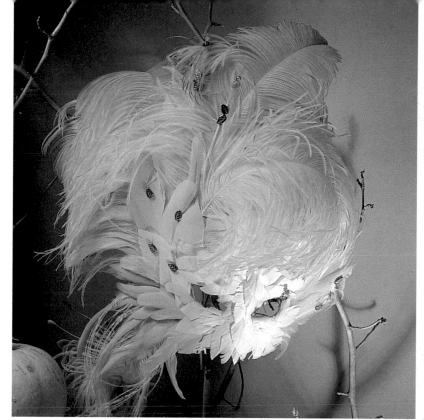

Masks by Danusia Brandstetter

ACTIVITIES

Elaborate ball gowns and immovable hairdos may leave your guests reluctant to undertake any activities that involve dexterity or even movement. Try some genteel amusements appropriate to the nature of the evening.

Try parlor games, such as Charades. Celebrity is an easy and amusing game you might try. Everyone writes the name of five (or more) celebrities on a slip of paper and drops the paper into a bowl. One person at a time, each player draws a name, then describes the celebrity to a partner without saying the celebrity name. The partner tries to guess the name based on the information provided. As the partner guesses correctly, the player continues to draw as many names as possible in a two- minute time period. The game continues until all the names have been selected. The team that guesses the most celebrity names wins.

PARTY FAVOR

As your satisfied guests start to drift toward the door at the end of the evening, remind them to take a party favor from a tiered tray on your table or sideboard.

Fill little white organdy gift bags (the kind used for wedding favors) with an assortment of the finer things in life (at least those that are tiny enough to fit in the bags). Let your guests pick which bag they like.

We stuffed these bags with luxurious chocolate coins, peppermint eggs, Italian hard candies, nostalgic rock candy, and pastel-colored bath beads. Stuff some bags with lavender or other fragrant herbs for an instant sachet that guests can slide into a drawer for a long-lasting reminder of your elegant Halloween affair.

DECADENT DESSERTS

CREAM CROWDIE

A *cranachan* or cream crowdie is a traditional Scottish dessert popular on Halloween night and used in divination games. When assembling the dessert, the host would insert coins, rings, and marbles into the mix. Those who got a coin would have a prosperous future, those who got a ring would get married, and those who got a marble were destined for a life of loneliness. If nothing was found in the dessert, the future was said to be uncertain. This dessert is sweet and a little bit decadent (note the whiskey) but very easy to make.

SERVES 6

YOU WILL NEED

6 TABLESPOONS (90 G) OATMEAL

1 PINT (900 G) RASPBERRIES OR STRAWBERRIES

20 OUNCES (591 ML) DOUBLE CREAM

6 TABLESPOONS (90 G) HONEY

6 TABLESPOONS (90 G) SINGLE MALT WHISKEY

MIXING BOWL

WHISK OR FORK

SAUCEPAN

PARFAIT GLASSES

TRINKETS TO MIX INTO DESSERTS SUCH AS, COINS, RINGS, OR MARBLES

1. Toast the oatmeal until it is golden brown. Let it cool in the pan.

2. Place the cream in a bowl and whisk until soft and relatively thick.

3. Add the honey and single malt whiskey and fold it in with a whisk until it's soft and creamy. If you're planning to add trinkets to the mixture, do it now.

4. Put a few raspberries in the bottom of each parfait glass. Fold the rest into the cream mixture.

5. Spoon the rest of mixture into the glasses, then add cream to the top and sprinkle on the oatmeal. Add a few more raspberries to the top and chill for three hours.

SOUL CAKES

YOU WILL NEED

2 sticks butter

3¾ cups sifted flour

1 cup (200 g) sugar

¼ teaspoon (1.2 ml) nutmeg or mace

1 teaspoon (5 g) each of cinnamon, ginger, and allspice

2 eggs

2 teaspoons (9.8 ml) malt vinegar or cider vinegar

Powdered sugar

Mixing bowl

Pastry blender (optional)

Fork

Baking sheet

In eighteenth and nineteenth century Ireland and England, women baked Soul Cakes on October 31 and November 1 in preparation for All Souls' Day, November 2. On All Souls' Day, children went from door to door "souling": singing and begging for soul cakes or, in some areas, exchanging soul cakes for candy or pennies. Later that night, families ate soul cakes after dinner and performed Souling Night plays.

Try making your own soul cakes on All Hallows' Eve using the following recipe.

1. Preheat the oven to 350° F (176°C).

2. Cut the butter into the flour with a pastry blender or fork.

3. Blend in the sugar, nutmeg, cinnamon, and allspice.

4. Beat the eggs in a separate bowl, then add in the vinegar. Add the egg mixture to the flour mixture and beat until a stiff dough forms.

5. Knead thoroughly and roll out, ¼ inch (6 mm) thick. Cut the dough into 3-inch (7.6 cm) rounds and set on a greased baking sheet.

6. Prick the top of the cakes with a fork. Bake for 20 to 25 minutes. Let cool and sprinkle with powdered sugar.

CHAMPAGNE PUNCH

As an elegant addition to your dessert table, try this rich champagne punch recipe.

In a bowl, combine the orange-flavored liqueur, the brandy, the black raspberry liqueur, and the pineapple juice and chill the mixture, covered, for at least 4 hours or overnight. In a large punch bowl, combine the chilled mixture with ginger ale and champagne and add ice cubes.

Makes about 16 cups (3.7 l), serving 12.

YOU WILL NEED

1 cup (236 ml) orange-flavored liqueur

1 cup (236 ml) brandy

½ cup (118 ml) black raspberry liqueur

2 cups (473 ml) unsweetened pineapple juice

1 quart (946.3) chilled ginger ale

2 chilled 750-ml bottles dry champagne

HALLOWEEN
on a
GRAND SCALE
City-wide Parties
& Festivals

If a small, stylish gathering is not your speed this Halloween, consider attending a gathering with a few thousand other Halloween enthusiasts. City-wide Halloween festivals are held all over the United States, and there are even some in England, too. Ranging from the spectacular to the absurd, here are a few of the more notable events you may want to investigate.

EERIE EVENTS OF SALEM, MASSACHUSETTS

Salem, of course, is infamous for its witch trials. Rather than fight its association with witchcraft, the city decided to embrace it (and indeed capitalize on it) by adopting the nickname Halloween City. An entire city block is transformed into a living ghost story for the Eerie Events festival. Eerie Events is a six-night party that includes reenactments, films, a bonfire, and concerts. The town's Peabody Essex Museum, comprised of historic houses and period gardens, hosts haunted tours and storytellers all in period costume telling chilling tales of ghostly happenings from the city's past.

GUAVAWEEN FESTIVAL, TAMPA, FLORIDA

Guavaween is billed as a "Latin-style Halloween," but may more closely resemble a New Orleans Mardi Gras. The festival gets its name from Tampa's nickname "the Big Guava," and is held in the city's historic district Ybor City, an area famous for its cigar factories. Guavaween was started in 1985 as a fundraiser and has now grown into an international event attended by over 100,000 people. During the day there are events for kids, but after dark it's strictly adults only. There is a parade called the "Mama Guava Stumble," hosted by the mythical Mama Guava, a costume contest, and concerts by big-name acts.

FANTASY FEST, KEY WEST FLORIDA

If you want to wear a barely-there costume this year, but don't want to shiver in the frosty fall temperatures, head to Key West for Fantasy Fest, the island's "adult only" Halloween festival. The free-spirited residents of Key West have never been known for a buttoned-up attitude. "Costumes" at Fantasy Fest may comprise of nothing more than a heavy coat of body paint applied with creative flair. Happenings include costume balls, beach games, a pet parade, and street parties. The event most closely resembles a Brazilian carnival, with elaborate floats, dramatic and fantastic costumes, and a hedonistic atmosphere.

THE HALLOWEEN FESTIVAL OF LONDON, ENGLAND

Every October 19-20, Queen Mary College in London hosts witches, druids, shamans, wiccans, odinists, and pagans of all traditions for a Halloween celebration. Festivities include a ritual involving pagan principles and a craft market. The party is split into different buildings named after pagan elements, earth, fire, water, air, and spirit. Music plays while people eat at the Cobweb Café. You may think they eat newts and tadpoles, but festivalgoers enjoy ordinary teas, coffee, juices, pies, and cream cakes.

THE PUMPKIN FESTIVAL OF KEENE, NEW HAMPSHIRE

Thousands of pumpkins glow on the main street of this quaint New England town as residents pursue their yearly goal of dominating the *Guinness Book of World Records* Most Lit Jack-O'Lanterns category. In 1991, the first year of the festival, participants brought 600 carved pumpkins that were displayed on a scaffold and lit. In 2000, the jack-o'lantern tally had reached 23, 727.

Happy Halloween!

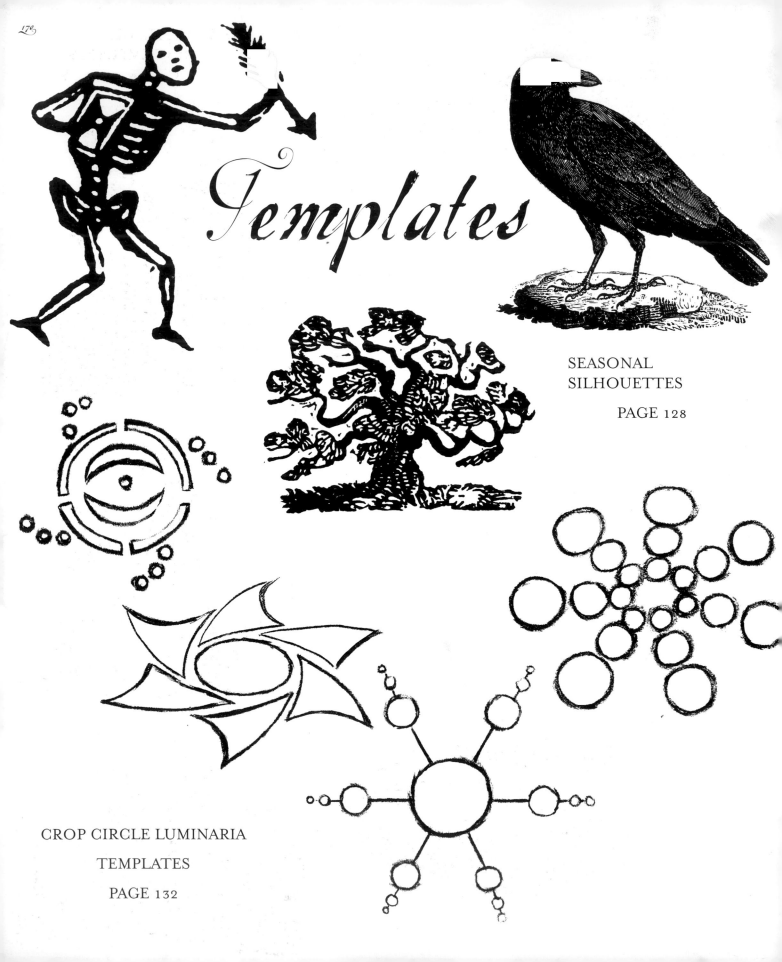

Templates

SEASONAL
SILHOUETTES

PAGE 128

CROP CIRCLE LUMINARIA

TEMPLATES

PAGE 132

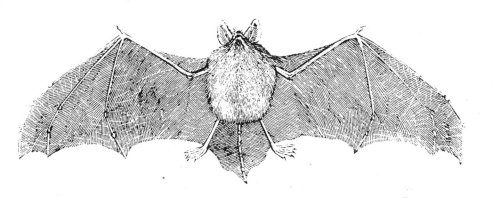

MASKED BALL INVITATION
ENVELOPE & MASK TEMPLATE

ENLARGE TO DESIRED SIZE

PAGE 162

CONTRIBUTING DESIGNERS

Danusia Brandstetter of Feathers by Danusia has been making feathered masks for almost 30 years. She started selling her feathered creations on the streets in San Francisco and is now one of the foremost feather-crafts experts in the United States. Each of her feathered masks is custom made in her studio and can contain from hundreds to thousands of feathers. Danusia and her family currently make their home in Portland, Oregon. Projects on page 163.

Casey Browning is a high school student who enjoys fashion design and volleyball. Her duct tape clothing has been featured in *WNC Parent*, a newspaper in Asheville, North Carolina. Projects on pages 32 to 35.

Barbara Evans creates dolls from handmade felt, found objects, natural materials, beads, and anything else with interesting texture, shape, and color. She served as technical consultant on Lark Book's *Creative Cloth Dolls* (2002). Projects on pages 124 to 127.

Trulee Grace Hall is a multimedia artist and musician who makes her home in the mountains of Asheville, North Carolina. Spanning the genres of visual, performing, and musical arts, Trulee's work includes calendar and greeting card production; furniture, clothing, and set design; interior decoration/restoration; fine arts painting and sculpture; video production; large-scale installation; and audio production and recording. Trulee also finds time to run a community art space in downtown Asheville, spotlighting the area's less conventional local talent. Projects on pages 12, 18, 28, 42, 44, 61, 64, 80 (wand) 94 (crown), 104, 116, 128.

Shaina Heller is an artist and performer based in Asheville, North Carolina. She is involved with Surreal Sirkus, a North Carolina performance and healing arts collective. Costume design is one of her favorite artistic outlets. Projects on pages 35 (neckbolts), 58, 67, 68.

Diana Light lives and works in the beautiful Blue Ridge Mountains of North Carolina. Her home studio, like her life, is surrounded by glittering glass in hundreds of forms, styles, and types. After earning her B.F.A. in painting and printmaking, she extended her expertise to etching and painting fine glass objects. She has contributed to numerous Lark books and is the co-author of Lark's *The Weekend Crafter: Etching Glass* (2000). Projects on pages 22, 24, 48(wig), 65, 66 (tail), 86, 92, 93(wig), 94, 132.

Ambra Lowenstein makes her home in the mountains of Asheville, North Carolina. She keeps a very busy schedule juggling her jobs as art teacher, acrobatics instructor, and performer. Ambra is a member of two performance groups—The Surreal Sirkus and Transform Venus. She does interpretive dance, aerial acrobatics, fire dancing, and, of course, lots of costume design. Projects on pages 96, 97, 100, 155 (horned mask), 156 (skull masks).

Christopher Mello is a gardener and sculptor based in Asheville, North Carolina. He encourages visitors to the area to stop by his garden and sculpture park, open to the public during daylight hours. Projects on pages 38, 130.

Joan K. Morris's artistic endeavors have led her down many successful creative paths. A childhood interest in sewing turned into professional costuming for motion pictures. After studying ceramics, Joan ran her own clay wind chime business for 15 years. Since 1993, Joan's Asheville, North Carolina coffeehouse, Vincent's Ear, has provided a vital meeting place for all varieties of artists and thinkers. Projects on pages 16, 20, 30, 36, 66 (pants), 48 (neck ruffles and cuffs), 74, 76, 78, 100, 102.

Joseph Peregine is an Atlanta-based painter and multimedia artist. He teaches art at Georgia State University. Projects on page 102.

Emma Pearson's creativity took her to Bretton Hall College in Leeds, England, where she received a B.A. with honors in art and design. After several art exhibits and years of design work, she started her own craft business in Wales. After moving to Asheville, North Carolina, in 2000, she created her own art and craft business, pellyfish.com. Her work incorporates the use of color, texture, decoration, recycled materials, and fun, and includes pieces which range from greeting cards to fleece wearables, and more. Projects on pages 26, 52.

Lois Simbach spent 10 years as a fashion designer in the garment industry, and five years as a costume designer, stylist, and model for theater, film, and television. She creates voodoo dolls, including a line of embellished soft sculpture dolls called Ju-Ju of the Vieux Carre. She now lives and works in Marshall, North Carolina. Projects on pages 60, 62, 88, 123.

Allison Smith is a craft designer who lives in Asheville, North Carolina, with her husband and four wonderful children. She enjoys reading, cooking, and traveling when she's not creating. Project on page 82.

Terry Taylor is an artist, jewelry designer, and crafter who lives in Asheville, North Carolina. Projects on pages 37, 98,99 (copyright-free image masks), 118, 136.

Tracy Thomson is a costume designer and miller who makes hats for all seasons and occasions. She owns and operates Kabuki Design Studio, located in New Orleans' historic French Quarter. You can see more of her hats, costumes, and accessories at her Web site, www.kabukihats.com. Project on page 95.

Nicole Tuggle is a mixed-media artist whose recent work has focused on collage and assemblage constructions. She finds beauty in found objects and old, neglected treasures. Check out more of her work at www.sigilation.com. Projects on page 142, 153, 162.

ACKNOWLEDGMENTS

Putting this book together was quite an experience—fun and challenging, but certainly never dull. Thanks to Deborah Morgenthal and Carol Taylor for giving me the opportunity. In their wisdom, they also teamed me with Susan McBride, whose design work on the book was absolutely visionary. Susan gave 200 percent to the book throughout the process, working tirelessly, with unflagging enthusiasm, and an unending stream of fresh, inspired ideas. This book was truly collaboration, and I could not have asked for a more perfect partner. Thanks to Rain Newcomb for sidebar research and writing, and Bev Jacobson for her expert proofing.

Thanks also to Keith Wright for his amazing photography, and Wendy Wright for always cheerfully pitching in to model and pull off any number of magical tricks of photography. It was a pleasure to work with this team, and the visuals are outstanding! Shannon Yokeley was also an invaluable addition to the design team, not only providing one-of-a-kind props and the perspective of a true Halloween lover, but being willing to run all manner of errand and carve some terrific pumpkins. Special thanks to Susan and Michael, Muriel Edens and Owen McMahon, Nicole and David, and Terry and Bitty for sharing their homes for the photo shoots. Stan and Jeff were always there for shuttling stuff to and fro and making sure we had whatwe needed. Ronnie Myers of Magnolia Beauregard supplied us with the wonderfully spooky mannequins. Thanks also to Dana Irwin for all the great props she provided.

All the designers who created the truly original costumes and other objects deserve a standing ovation for their efforts (see page 172 for more information about them). Each time new costumes or decorative item arrived, the whole building was amazed and delighted by the results. Special thanks to Terry and Joanie for responding quickly to last-minute requests for this and that. Our models were such good sports! They are: Vern (the Queen of Everything) and Hannes (the dejected drone and boring mask guy), Rain (the scary snow woman and samurai), Trulee (the French poodle and spider), Casey (Mrs. Frankenstein), Wendy (oh so many things), Annie and Christopher (Mother Earth and the Green Man), Tom (the Gladiator and masked guy), Lorelei (tropical showgirl), Megan (bored partygoer in mask), Duncan (photo booth guy), and Allison (photo booth gal). Thanks for lending your good looks and attitude to bring the costumes to life.

Finally, thank you to Andrew for all his support at home during all those extra hours I spent working on the book. I truly couldn't have done it without you.

Index